## Praise for Tran
## The Hypnotic Art of Lea

CW01661757

*This book is so simple and fun to ... and analogies. Whether you are a hypnotherapy beginner or an advanced trainer you will enjoy every paragraph of it.*

*As someone who knows Karen's amazing lively and straight forward style, I was hearing her voice as I was reading the Trance Dance.*

*Where many would think that it is all about the therapist's skills, Karen gave the expression "it takes two to tango" a new dimension, by highlighting the importance of guidance through the Hypnotic Art of Leading and Following to insure a client centered approach in an amazingly written style.*

***— Daniel Ghanimé, The Control Alternative***

*The Trance Dance, The Hypnotic Art of Leading and Following is a must read for all new hypnotherapists. It picks up where your education left off. Here you are armed with strategies and some level of understanding in regard to what you are going to do with who-ever walks in your door. It is a bit daunting at first. Then you find out fast, that there is no such thing as a text-book case. Each person comes to you already in their own trance. Your job is to disassociate them from the negative trance and associate them into the positive trance they are asking for. This often results in choosing to go the "finding the right script" way. This doesn't help you to use the important information your client is giving you and it often doesn't lead to real change.*

*Karen, in her easy, fun, articulate way, helps you to understand that each client comes to you with all the information you need to help them be successful in getting their needs met. Understanding this and believing this at a core level allows you to really listen to your client. And that is where the dance begins. Karen gives you a way of seeing and thinking that can be used with any methodology/strategy you choose. The ones she shares are timeless and offer a structure that is easy to work with and will result in success for your client and you.*

*Karen is a master of language and offers you valuable insights and creative ways of thinking about hypnosis. It's a quick read and a valuable one too.*

***— Laney Coulter, BCH, CI, NLP, M.Ed Loving Kindness Hypnosis***

*Karen is a natural instructor, very positive and a-matter-of-fact type attitude allows people to look at things as if it's not complicated. Karen's down-to earth attitude gives people a comfort in accepting what she says.*

***— Carm Blacconiere, BCH, OB, Chairman, Mid-America Hypnosis Conference***

*So true to her gift, Karen speaks her teachings in an engaging, direct, and conversational way, as if you're sitting across the table from her chatting over coffee. What's magical about her presentation of the Trance Dance is that instead of the dance floor being small and limited like the ones in cocktail lounges, she gifts us with the grand spaciousness of a brilliantly-designed ballroom. Highly recommended!*

***— Suzy Day, Clinical & Spiritual Hypnotherapist CCHt, MHC, MBWP***

*Trance Dance is spectacular! The title and chapter headings tell a story that made my artistic heart happy and the material is organized in such a way that it's useful for both the beginner and the seasoned hypnotist. I am a long-time fan of all Karen Hand works, but this book truly over delivers with techniques, insights, NLP presuppositions/explanations, and even transcripts. I simply could not put this book down!*

***— Ashley Lynn Caputo, Certified Clinical/Medical Hypnotherapist, Neurofeedback Trainer, Reiki Master, Student Yoga Therapist***

# Trance Dance

## The Hypnotic Art of Leading and Following

Karen Hand

Trance Dance- The Hypnotic Art of Leading and Following

ReMind Publishing. Chicago, IL 

ISBN: 978-0-9992589-2-7

Edited by Kelly Joy Simmons

*“Most people walk through the world in a trance of disempowerment. Our work is to transform that into a trance of empowerment."*

**— Dr. Milton H. Erickson**

# THE DANCE CARD

# FOREWARD

Some hypnotists seem to have two left feet. But it's not their fault…

I grew up in the early sixties. In the age when teenagers were becoming "cool". It was all about making the scene. The music was hopping and Elvis had shaken his hips, and we all knew that dancing was the doorway to "groovy" … but I just couldn't get it. I was stiff and awkward and uncomfortable and my watusi looked more like a seizure than a dance. I was incredibly self conscious and concerned that anyone seeing me would think that I was an idiot … or even worse KNOW it.

Then two important things happened. My sister started teaching me to dance and some of my more patient friends took pity on me and showed me some moves … and as I enjoyed being with them I relaxed … and discovered that dancing could be a pleasant social interaction to share with someone … rather than an awkward performance being offered for their judgment. Rather than two of us - each trying to determine the best way to get around the floor and each having our own dance … it was something that happened quite naturally when we took the chance of dancing together. It wasn't about the technique. It was about the interaction between the dancers. A special way of being together. Intimate and authentic, each with their own style, yet comfortably within the guidelines set by social convention and (as millennia of history show us) the rhythm of the drum.

Milton Erickson once said, “Hypnosis is a relationship.”

It is a shared experience between client and practitioner who, when in sync with one another, are a team of creative artists in motion – stepping and gliding gracefully in a rich and transformational waltz. That's what this book is about.

As I said, “Some hypnotists seem to have two left feet ... but it's not their fault.”

I got past my two left feet when I got some good instruction...and was encouraged to worry less about being judged and to enjoy creating a connection. Dancing wasn't about ME...it was about US. In the beginning, many hypnotists have gotten the idea that it's about “putting someone under” and “giving them suggestions” and they judge themselves and the entire process on their ability to achieve a result in that way. It's not their fault...they just need a teacher, a friend.

It wasn't until someone pointed out what would become obvious. A good dance partner is a collaborator who encourages and supports the best from the other ... who helps the other to showcase their special skills ... to become better and better all the time. And the most important lesson of all—that dancing was a CELEBRATION.

This book sounds a wakeup call for all hypnotists about the partnerships we enter into with our clients (and everyone else) every day. You've had your lessons, now let Karen Hand show you what she knows so well. In this pleasant, casual and friendly volume, you'll find all the encouragement and all the tools that you need to dance the Trance Dance..

**— Michael Watson, CMT, President - Hypnosis Education Association, Principal Trainer - International Association of Counselors and Therapists, Founder - Phoenix Services, Orlando, Florida**

# PREFACE

Have you ever wondered if you have what it takes to help your clients solve their problems? Have you worried that you might run out of ideas or suggestions? What happens if you make the wrong suggestion?

How much time have you spent looking for or writing the "perfect" script only to discover that your client didn't give you all the information in the screening? Or perhaps a client calls for an appointment wanting help with confidence, but once inside the office admits what they really need help with is erectile dysfunction! Maybe your "confidence script" will still work...and then again, maybe not.

You may have already noticed, I ask a lot of questions. And you should too! THAT'S the map to session success. The right questions will let you know exactly what to do with your client in your session. This book will show you the questions AND what to listen/look for in the answers.

Do you spend way too many hours predicting what might happen when the client arrives and preparing for that prediction? If so, you've spent way too many hours wasting your precious time!

Unless, of course, you're an exceptionally accurate psychic; then maybe THAT'S what you should be selling! If not, this book is for you.

If you ever harbor guilt for guessing wrong or if you have any feelings of being responsible for your client's success, this book is for you. If you've been told to listen to the client, but you haven't been told what to listen for, this book is for you. If you are at all intrigued right now, and want to keep reading, this book is for you!

When I was a baby hypnotist, I often heard experienced hypnotists say, "The client will tell you exactly what to do and say to make the change that makes the difference." And that's true. Unfortunately, most hypnotists are not trained in what to listen for or what to do with that information once you have it. This book will bridge that gap.

As you read, notice yourself being hypnotized along the way with some experiential learning. It might happen with the words...or maybe it's the stories...then again it might be the metaphors or the transcript of a session demo. You'll find a variety of hypnotic teaching tools woven throughout these pages. And you're likely to be amazed at how quickly you decide to go looking for tips, tricks and techniques you can immediately add to your sessions. Starting now.

# INTRODUCTION

This book will enable you to connect the dots between Hypnosis Training and Session Success. And it will answer the question about exactly what to listen for and how to turn that information into a successful change session using NLP, Hypnosis, Persuasive Conversation and/or Direct Suggestion both in desultory conversation and in deep trance states. I call the process the **Hypnotic Trance Dance for Positive Change**.

The Hypnotic Trance Dance is a combo step that starts by finding out what the client already believes and then discovering what they need to learn to create the successful outcome they've hired you to achieve.

It has been said that NLP is "wide-awake hypnosis." And it is! In the same sense that all persuasive speech is wide-awake hypnosis. The truth is, hypnosis happens whether the eyes are closed or open, whether a person is relaxed or in a state of tension. Hypnosis happens because the mind is always making adjustments. Just like the tiny adjustments a driver continuously makes behind the wheel, the mind is constantly maneuvering to stay on path with the currently operating belief system.

You might wonder at my use of the modifier "currently" when discussing the operating belief system. Beliefs are fluid because a belief is not fact. It is...belief. A belief is based on what you've been told and what you've experienced. But it is definitely not necessarily a fact! Beliefs can and do change. Just the same, people always act and behave in a way that matches their own currently operating B. S. (Belief System).

Client Connie is an easy example. Connie is a friendly and extroverted leader of a non-profit organization. She easily conducts meetings and fundraising events with aplomb. But when it comes to her own self-esteem and personal financial success, she falls short of her goals. Connie believed the problem started all the way back when she graduated from kindergarten. She remembered tiny diplomas on a little table in the front of the room and all the kids walked up one by one to get theirs. When Connie's name was called, she excitedly jumped up out of her chair, running to the front of the room. Just as she got to the teacher, Connie tripped and bumped the table. All the diplomas went rolling to the floor. Connie's teacher said, "Well, we're on a roll now!" The parents and other kids burst into laughter. Connie was embarrassed because everyone laughed at her. (At least she BELIEVED they were laughing at her).

I asked, "I wonder if anyone showed concern or asked if you were okay?"

Connie lowered her head and said, "No, they just laughed at me."

"Isn't that odd behavior? For caring adults?" I inquired. "To laugh at an innocent five-year-old? I wonder if they could have been laughing at the teacher's quick-witted comment."

After all, Connie had remembered that "embarrassing" quip all these years later. Maybe that's what sent the adults into laughter rather than the tumbling child. And now we're beginning to challenge the BELIEF around that event.

I continued musing, "I wonder if that's the very day you learned your actions may be watched, even judged. And I wonder if that's the day your subconscious mind decided to hone your skills at comedic timing, clever responses, and turning any occurrence into part of the show."

Connie naturally did an internal search and found evidence of her own witty ability to keep the show going no matter what happens. Connie also realized in that review that it was the day she set up internal strategies to be exceedingly strict with her behavior and always strive for perfection to avoid being the brunt of a joke.

There had been two lessons in that one early childhood event, however, Connie had been focusing on the negative revelation of being judged instead of the entire overall experience. That same event may have also "gifted" Connie with the behaviors that made her perfectly matched for each career she'd chosen in life as she had re-invented herself beautifully through three career changes. A few well-placed questions did some instant reframing. And the dance toward a much more positive self-image continued.

As we move through this book, you'll discover a simple questionnaire that reveals the client's desired outcome of the session, the limiting beliefs that have been standing in the way of success, the leverage for change, the suggestions that will create success, and exactly what techniques to use in wide awake persuasive conversation or in deep trance hypnosis. In NLP training, it's called the Outcome Specification Exercise. In the real world, I call it an Outcome Specification Intervention. You will soon see how it takes a client from problem mindset to successful mindset in eight easy steps/questions. And you will see how it is Trance-Formational!

The questions, by the way, are a guideline to reveal information. We'll explore them in depth along with a demonstration. I've included a transcript from an Outcome Intervention demo, annotated to highlight the findings. You can also watch a video of the demo at KarenHand.com/Trance-Dance. You'll see some instant inner child work, a tip for some parts therapy and more.

But, before we get to the questions, the Hypnotic Trance Dance involves the frame you take into the session. I once heard cutting edge hypno expert Melissa Tiers say, "If you can't see your client successful, get out of the room, because you're not helping." I couldn't agree more. So, we'll start with some pre-framing to get your mindset ready for success. There will also be lots of helpful tips along the way for you to adapt to your own style and level of expertise.

And while we will be exploring a line of questioning that often leads to change in a one-session wonder, it is also designed to gather information that you can use for all subsequent sessions with your client. Sometimes a series of sessions, accountability and coaching is necessary to facilitate the change. When you arm yourself with a wide variety of Trance Dance steps, you'll expedite bringing out the best in your clients. Now as we traverse this dance floor, let me lead. You will discover how easy it is to follow!

CHAPTER 1:

# TAP INTO THE MAGIC

You're probably aware of the television program Dancing With The Stars. Professional ballroom dancers are paired with celebrities of varying dance experience and the teams compete for a mirror-ball trophy. The dancers work for several weeks with their celebrity partners to gauge their ability and teach them steps for the elimination-style weekly competition.

The dance pros have to: discover what their celebrity is capable of doing; teach new movements; grow their partner's performance ability; and choreograph a series of numbers that will utilize both old and newly acquired abilities.

Of course, the celebs who have the most dance experience and rhythmic ability have a distinct advantage, but in reality, some fairly uncoordinated celebrities have advanced quite far and have even won the competition. And even though the celebrity takes home the trophy, it is their pro who gets the credit for being able to bring out the celebrity's inner resources to help them look and perform their best.

The dancing professionals on that show cannot MAKE someone be a dancer. But they can help build new skills and bring out the most that their celebrity has to offer. Does that seem familiar?

You, as a hypnotist, hypnotherapist, coach, teacher, mentor, etc., have much in common with the dance pros on Dancing With The Stars. Your job is to discover where your client is today, what resources they have on which to build, what new skills can be taught, and how to bring out the very best that they already have inside of them for the goal they want to reach.

Do you remember the old movie The Miracle Worker with Patti Duke starring as Helen Keller? In the pivotal scene, the teacher Annie Sullivan (played by Anne Bancroft) and Helen are at a well pumping water and Annie finally got through to Helen. Helen suddenly comprehended what Annie had been trying to teach her as Annie held Helen's hand in the water. After much fighting and stress, for the first time, Helen understood that those odd shapes Annie was making in her palm actually had meaning. This new comprehension brought Helen out of her silent darkness, expanded her world and her choices. Helen wanted to learn more and more with this connection to the outside. Suddenly she felt empowered. She felt as if she could connect with anything in the outside world.

Remember back to when you learned something new. Maybe it was riding a bike or skating or even as far back as walking or talking or eating with a spoon; your new skill empowered you to take on the world in a new and different way.

My friend, Chicago Hypnotist Larry Garrett, often jokes that when he first started as a hypnotist, he was far more confident than he is now. Back then, he thought hypnosis could do anything! He knew the right words and some fancy techniques and he was a showman. Larry took the stage and did a number of great performances with his audiences. Until one day his techniques didn't work. His show fell flat. Larry went from fearless to cautious and insecure in one night.

Fortunately, Larry didn't let it stop him. He replayed the evening in his mind and discovered how a turn of phrase can make all the difference in the world. He perfected his language. And he continued to learn.

Larry has been a hypnotist since 1968. He opened his first office in Chicago in 1970. He continues, even after all this time, to attend conferences and to sit in on lectures from other hypnotists both new and seasoned. Larry opens his lovely wellness center on the first Sunday of every month to anyone who wants to discover something about hypnosis or wellness. He encourages everyone to talk about their services, workshops, classes, and gatherings. It took a while to get through to my Type-A competitive spirit that there is enough business for all of us! But eventually I learned that we each attract the client who is right for us. Sometimes I refer clients to Larry, sometimes he refers to me. Larry keenly knows that we are continuously learning, growing and refining. There's no end to the ways we can get better and better.

When I started my first hypnosis business, I was armed with a bookshelf full of scripts and a plan to help people lose weight, quit smoking and break bad habits. I believed I could help everyone! I remember walking up to smokers on cold Chicago street corners offering my business card as I smiled broadly and said, "I can help you quit that!" And I knew that I could! I was surprised that I was not greeted by sighs of relief and requests to make an appointment.

It took a little while for the reality to set in that even the best hypnotist in the world can't make someone do something they don't want to do.

Understand, covert hypnosis certainly exists. People accept suggestions continuously that fit in with their desires and their core values. In fact, the number one hypnotist in the world is the television set. Think about the trance state we enter as we sit "mindlessly" (without resistance) staring at the TV or computer screen or any form in which we interact with a social media outlet.

Realize any suggestion can be easily compounded when delivered by your friends or trusted authorities or when you experience it as something that is congruent with your beliefs.

Also remember that a belief is not always a fact – it may be factual, but a belief is just as likely to appear to be fact just because you and other like-minded individuals believe it to be true. Once upon a time everyone believed the world was flat. Spoiler Alert: The earth was just as round then as it is now. The commonly held belief did not make the belief factual, but those holding that belief automatically acted and behaved as if it were fact.

Of course, people differ in their beliefs. Take the Vikings, for example. They never would have sailed off for a new world if they truly believed they were going to fall off the edge. And just like that, the Vikings and other exploring adventurous voyagers were able to change the belief simply by returning safely. It is that easy to change a belief when one is open to discovering new information.

New information is part of our dance. In this book, I intend to share the secrets that set me free in my hypnosis travels, and, opened the path to help others change for good.

Understand, my training has gone far beyond the initial certification. Just like Larry Garrett, I continue to attend trainings and conferences. I am a member of several social media forums. Each is an outlet for learning a turn of phrase, a new idea, a different way of going about something.

I have no intention of making you a carbon copy of me! I'm enough. And you are enough. What I do intend to do is offer some tips for running smooth and successful sessions. Take the information that resonates with you and adapt it to your style. The clients you have attracted are with you because they BELIEVE you can help them. I'm hoping this book gives you the confidence to also deeply and completely BELIEVE YOU CAN HELP THEM!

I sense you are ready.

CHAPTER 2:

# GET ON THE DANCE FLOOR

Since this is a dance, let's be on the same dance floor.

These are my BELIEFS about hypnosis. And just as in any other persuasive encounter, you are entitled to take my suggestions and add them to your toolkit...or leave them. I will not follow you around and demand that you use my techniques nor will I claim that my technique is superior to any other successful session strategy. I won't even tell you that this session outline will work every time for every client. What I will do is share what works for me in some form in almost every session. All I ask is that you take what is valuable to you and make it your own!

Hypnosis is easy! Hypnosis happens all the time. In fact, it's far easier to be in a trance state than it is to be totally conscious and present. We often have to really work for conscious awareness while we're easily going into and out of trance states all day (and all night) long. Dreams are the way that the subconscious mind (SCM) categorizes and processes events. Daydreams are trance states that you actually sometimes catch yourself experiencing. And you may be aware of many other trance states such as:

- Highway Hypnosis
- Television Trance
- Girlfriends-at-Lunch Trance
- Alone-with-the-Husband Trance
- Making-Dinner-for-the-Family Trance
- Teaching Trance
- Learning Trance
- Going-to-Church Trance
- Avoidance Trance
- Binge-eating Trance
- Shower Trance
- Smoking Trance
- Waiting-in-the-doctor's-lobby trance
- Etc., Etc., Etc. Hypnotic Trance

You're in a trance state when you always remember to react negatively at the sight of a spider or the sound of someone's voice. It's an entirely different trance state when you're hiking through a beautiful forest. But that could turn into a different automatic trance if you suddenly discover you're lost in the woods. We go in and out of trance states all day long without external suggestion. AND WE'RE GOOD AT IT! Naturally and automatically!

Those are "accidental" hypnotic states. We move in and out of them without much conscious awareness. We can be hypnotized by the ropes and stanchions showing us how to line up at the bank or at an amusement park ride.

As with ANY hypnotic suggestion, the "line up here" suggestion can be taken or ignored. Someone who walks into the bank in the "I-need-to-cash-this-check-with-the-teller" trance is likely to follow the obvious direct suggestion for the preferred route to get there and get in the sectioned off waiting line.

Someone in the "I'm-not-sure-who-can-help-me" trance is just as likely to bypass the formalities of the line and walk right up to a teller saying, "Quick question, who do I see about a mortgage loan?" That customer may have simply negatively hallucinated the direct suggestion in the middle of the room – the telltale indicators of how to wait in the line. Negative hallucination is not seeing something that's in plain sight. It's a deep level of hypnosis on Harry Aron's Depth Scale. And it happens without the explicit expertise of a trained hypnotist.

We can be hypnotized by a single bold colored carpet square on the floor or a masking tape X or any indicator of where to stand while you wait in line. If you walk in with an intended outcome of quick service, you see it as an easy suggestion to take. If you enter in some other kind of trance, you may not even see the suggestion for where to line up. It's a suggestion that can be easily taken or ignored/negatively hallucinated.

Negative hallucination happens when one notices a cut or bruise and wonders when THAT happened! Whenever that injury occurred, the receiver was in such a deep state of trance with whatever they were doing at the time, they didn't even notice direct harm to their body. Someone deeply engrossed in a sporting event on TV may not hear their name called by someone in the same room. Some call that "selective hearing," but I call it negatively hallucinating the obvious auditory interruption.

Same thing happens with positive hallucination. That's seeing something that is not there. It happens in relationships all the time. Many years ago, a friend introduced me to her fiancé, and it was immediately apparent that they were not at all right for each other. That was long before I was a hypnotist or knew how to understand the mind games we play on ourselves and each other. Hindsight being 20/20, I now realize they were both in the "I'm-ready-to-get-married-and-be-recognized-as-an-adult" trance. Nothing was going to stop the Trance Dance they were doing together.

Once the "I do's" were said, they quickly knew they were not a good match. After getting what they both wanted by crossing the threshold of "adulthood," this couple realized they weren't in it until death parted them. They stayed married for less than a year and consciously uncoupled in a rather friendly divorce. Each eventually found their way to happier partnerships.

My friend and her short-term spouse had wanted to be grown up and respected as adults so they thought getting married was the way to accomplish that goal. They had positively hallucinated a rosy future while negatively hallucinating any signs of problems. It happens in all sorts of relationships all the time.

And all of that tends to be accidental hypnosis. We mastermind those trance states in our own head, collecting information that supports our desired outcome and ignoring information to the contrary.

See? Hypnosis is easy!

I am sure you see it all the time. When you become a Certified Hypnotist and people hire you to facilitate change, that's when it becomes "on-purpose" hypnosis. Your client is there waiting for you to "do something to them." And now you are both on the same dance floor.

## CHAPTER 3:

# BASIC STEPS

All dances have basic steps and the Hypnotic Trance Dance is no different. It's quite simple really. The analogy I use most often these days when thinking about (or explaining) how the mind works is the Cell Phone Metaphor.

When we get a new cellphone, it comes with a fully functioning operating system pre-bundled with a phone, a camera, an email program, spell check and some operational things that we will probably never even notice. The longer we have the phone, the more personalized it becomes. You might add a special screen picture, a case, and probably a bunch of apps. It's the apps that are most intriguing to me.

As humans, we plop out of the birth canal pre-bundled with a bunch of cool operations. We can breathe, blink, startle, swallow, suck, digest food, learn vast amounts of new information, etc. That's our Operating System. And we're already pre-loaded with a desire and ability to survive which allows us to learn new things that also become automatic.

Do you remember learning to walk? Probably not, but only you could do it, no one could do it for you. You accepted the assist of a table leg or adult hand, but you had to discover how to walk on your own. You kept trying until YOU DISCOVERED BALANCE! Soon you were walking all over the place. And having balance came in pretty handy years later when you learned to ride a bike. All of those skills and abilities are stored in your Subconscious Mind, the vast memory card that holds all of our apps such as values, behaviors, imagination, beliefs, favorite color, address, etc.

Additional apps are added as necessary.

Remember Connie who took a tumble in front of everyone in kindergarten and felt judged? At that young age, she downloaded the "perfectionist" app designed to protect her from feeling those negative feelings in the future. That behavior app has worked remarkably well to help her work hard and succeed. It also works well to keep her stressed and to prevent her from recognizing "good enough." At the same time, she downloaded the judgement app she perceived and started using it regularly on herself and others. (Perfectionists often expect as much from others as they do from themselves and they will ALWAYS disappoint themselves).

I often ask clients what they do when they've discovered an app on their phone doesn't really work as they had expected. Sometimes the client will say they delete it. That's good! Some clients say they just leave the app and never open it again. That's not so good, but it's GREAT information to me as hypnotist. And it opens the door for a discussion about old programs running in the background that use up battery life and are always at the ready to jump in if possible. Then, the dance (as always) is to discover what works...and what doesn't work...and do the necessary fine-tuning.

Back to the phone analogy, the Unconscious Mind (UM), in this metaphor, is the Operating System. Sometimes the Operating System (blood pressure, hot flashes, etc.) needs attention and that's where we place the focus. But mostly, we work in the realm of belief which is found in the SCM right next to imagination and they go hand-in-hand for easy change work.

The Conscious Mind (CM) is the operator. Data entry. The CM is the most limited in terms of abilities and the most opinionated. Some hypnotists endeavor to get around the CM or close it down/lock it out. I happen to enjoy the CM and invite it to participate in all activities whether as an observer or a participant when needed. After all, it is the CM that scheduled and paid for the appointment. I believe in "dancing with the one that brung me."

All of the levels of the mind are doing their best for our benefit. I've even been known to call upon The Cloud, that vast Super Conscious (SC) level of knowledge that can tap into anything the client believes in outside of themselves. Angels, guides, wisdom and intuition lie outside the physical confines of the phone and its operator. Sometimes in the dance it's the client who's doing the imagining and sometimes the hypnotist is using their imagination for a change.

Remember, the only limits are the limits placed by your own beliefs and imagination. On Dancing With The Stars, they do the Salsa, Tango, Waltz, Foxtrot, Mambo, and more. What do you believe you can do with the Hypnotic Trance Dance?

CHAPTER 4:

# PRE-SUPPOSE A GREAT PARTNER

Early in my hypnotist career, I believed I'd learned a magic modality that could fix anything! When a prospective client inquired about an issue, I was taught to say, "Sure, I can do that. I do it all the time!" I'm guessing it's that kind of training that has so many new hypnotists on social media platforms asking for scripts or techniques that can help a client who's coming in tomorrow/next week.

It also puts a lot of pressure on the hypnotist to be the "answer woman" or "wizard." Soon, but not quite yet, we'll get to those "magic questions" that can make the change feel like magic.

(Notice the building anticipation!) But, another spoiler alert, it isn't really magic. It's actually the strategic application of conversational hypnosis/NLP (Neuro-linguistic Programming). And the full explanation is coming up shortly. But first, let's reduce the responsibility and expand the mind with some wonderful things to know about clients and all humans in general.

We're told to avoid assumptions because, well, you know, when we assume it makes an ass out of u and me. But **supposing** is just fine! As a matter of fact, the NLP presuppositions set me (and my change work) free.

Take a couple of NLP classes or read a couple of NLP books and you're likely to get several different lists of Presuppostions. I will share the "beliefs" that made a difference for me. If you run across other examples with useful beliefs, I certainly wouldn't stop you from adding them to your list.

Discover how powerful this framework can be when applied to each of your clients and notice how it can transform your stress into useful curiosity. You may find yourself having much more fun with your clients no matter what issue they bring to the session.

1. **There is no failure, only feedback.**

   I list this presupposition first because it's a valuable life lesson going far beyond facilitating hypnosis sessions.

   My dogs have been great examples of this. We obviously don't speak the same language, and perhaps that makes it easier to put together a cohesive dance since we know from the beginning that it's a discovery process. The sweetest dog I ever had was Cocoa, a Shepherd/Collie mix. On a long trip when she was fairly young, we stopped at a McDonald's and Cocoa got a McD's cheeseburger without the mustard and ketchup. It was gone in a flash. Everything except the pickle. She spit out the pickle!

   That was some great feedback! We didn't feel as if we'd failed our dog. We chuckled at her obvious food preferences and the next time she got a cheeseburger as a treat, it was ordered PLAIN...no pickle!

   When you are doing the hypnotic dance, you take a step and then observe the client's reaction. No matter what the reaction is, you get valuable feedback to determine the next step.

Let's take the simple eye-lock suggestibility test. You know it. "Relax your eyelids so much that they just won't work." You can do the best patter and suggestion and the client might still open their eyes when you say, "Try to open them and find you cannot."

RELAX! It's only feedback. And when you realize that's just feedback, it's easy to keep your cool and offer this step: "That's great! You just proved you can open your eyes. I wonder if this time you can RELAX your eyes so much they just stay closed. Because, you know, you have to tense your eyelid muscles in order to open them. Now that you've proven to yourself that you always have control, what happens when YOU RELAX YOUR EYELIDS so much, they just want to stay closed. Only you can do it, no one can do it for you."

Then you wait for the next piece of feedback. Be ready to stay on your toes and dance! In all sorts of persuasive communication, keep an open mind, take the feedback and look for the win-win situation.

2. **We are always communicating.** -OR- **We are all ways communicating.**

If someone asks you a question and you sit stoically without answering, that's communication. If you walk up half a flight of stairs and lose your breath, that's communication from your body. A smile, a nod, a cough, a brightly colored scarf, tennis shoes, blond hair, bright red lipstick, a tattoo, cold hands, a warm drink...they are all forms of non-verbal COMMUNICATION.

The actual words we use are simply codes to get our thoughts into someone else's head. (If you want to know more about strategically using words to persuade, read my book **Magic Words and Language Patterns, The Hypnotist's Essential Guide to Crafting Irresistible Suggestions**.) The vast SCM is scanning for more than words. It reads communication with the senses and intuition.

-AND-

**The meaning of the communication is in the response you get.**

If you hire someone to paint your garage door green and tell them to pick up paint on the way over to your house, you've left a lot to interpretation. You certainly have a green color in your mind's eye. You might have clearly pictured a dark forest green, but you can't complain too much when the painter applies a neon lime green color to your garage. The response indicates you left it up to the painter to choose the green!

Both elements of communication, what you're communicating and the response you get, are important to understand.

Your tone, tempo, volume, gestures, eye movements, posture, etc., are even more important to any communication than the actual words used to deliver your message. Some say the words account for about seven percent of the message being delivered. Words certainly have power, but it is the response to the words that indicates what has been received/communicated.

Have you ever seen someone say something and when it's misunderstood they use the exact same words (maybe louder) to try again? If the message is still misunderstood, the speaker might even become frustrated or get angry with the listener. This happens often in relationship (husband/wife, parent/child, boss/employee, etc.)

conversations. We have a natural tendency to believe whatever we're thinking is the right thing to think so everyone else must be thinking the same thing. Unfortunately, that delusional line of thinking rules out each person's uniqueness.

When you understand the dance of communication, you realize that if a response is different from what you expect, it would be crazy to try the same thing again and expect a different result. In the case of the house painter, before you send him back to the paint store for a different color, you might choose to be more specific, maybe even google paint colors and find the exact stock code for the color YOU have in mind.

Take the feedback, adjust as necessary and then try something different.

3. **If something isn't working, try anything else.**

I've already mentioned the insanity of continuing to do the same thing while expecting a different result. The same applies to your techniques and to your clients.

A progressive muscle relaxation may work beautifully with your first five clients. And then you find yourself using the same induction for the sixth client only to discover they start to fidget and wiggle their fingers. That could be some great feedback that relaxation isn't occurring with this technique for this client. That's when it's important to move on and try anything different. Something different will at least give you a different result.

I once had a smoking cessation client who complained of restless legs. Sara claimed the moment she tilts back in a recliner, her legs start to shake and she can't stand it. She said that even sitting will make her legs shake after a few minutes. I calmly wondered what Sara's legs do while she's standing and she said that's when she's the most relaxed. So, I shrugged my shoulders and invited her to stand next to the wall where she could lean if she needed any physical support. Sara wanted to slowly taper off from a 40-year smoking habit. She quit smoking in four sessions, all of them standing/leaning against a wall.

Sara came back to me several months later wondering if we could do anything about her restless legs and that's when we worked on relaxation. You see, Sara didn't ask me for "relaxation" when she hired me for smoking cessation so there was no need to waste time on what she hadn't asked for then. I facilitated what she asked for – quitting smoking – and that gave her the confidence to return when she was ready to make the next change.

By the way, progressive muscle relaxation was not the key. When we gave Sara's legs "a voice" in some parts work, she discovered her legs really wanted to move more than she was giving them the opportunity to do throughout the day. So, she stopped believing that her life was limited by her "condition" of restless legs. Instead, she decided she had control over that condition. Dissociating from the diagnosis, she experimented with walking during the day. Sara started with short trips and rapidly extended her walks. In her second session for restless legs, she said she was "listening" to her legs. And if they started to jump, she stood up and gave them some exercise. Sara noted that her legs were getting "less restless" every day plus she was sleeping comfortably through the night.

I wonder what changes might have been lost if I had insisted on doing hypnosis the way it had always worked with all previous clients.

**4. The one with the most flexibility of thought and action**

**is the one most likely to succeed. (The law of "Requisite Variety")**

Imagine yourself driving toward an unmarked intersection at the exact same time as two other cars, each coming from different directions. The driver who is flexible enough to slow down and stop while the other cars cross the intersection is the one least likely to have a damaged car.

The hypnotist who can flexibly dance to a different drummer is the one who's most likely to help the widest variety of clients.

Throughout my career, I've learned a number of "systems" for successful hypnosis. And I've given several the benefit of the doubt. Admittedly, sometimes I stuck to a system or protocol even though it wasn't actually working for "everyone on everything" as I'd been promised.

Turns out, that was great FEEDBACK to discover that systems and protocols sell for instructional purposes. But in the actual work of hypnosis, I've found only a few clients who truly are "textbook" cases. The majority of people have their own unique set of nuances and circumstances that may require a change or two in the dance step. A beautifully written guided visualization process may not work well with a client who prefers an auditory or kinesthetic representational system. You can ditch the script or protocol and go client-centered with an individualized approach, or you can spend/waste time and effort teaching a client how to visualize while not addressing the issue for which you were hired. I find it much more useful to practice requisite variety and have a repertoire of responses for whatever feedback a client may provide.

Thinking back now, my favorite toy as a toddler was a brightly colored three-dimensional wooden mailbox with some wooden pieces to insert in various openings. The goal, of course, was to get all of the pieces into the mailbox for the sheer joy of opening the door at the base so the pieces could be retrieved and the game repeated.

I experienced the law of requisite variety while learning the square block was never going to go through that round hole. Flexibility was the key to getting all those various pieces into the box. And flexibility is a key ingredient in the Trance Dance.

5. **Choice is better than no choice.** -AND- **People always make the best choice available to them at the time.**

   As Maya Angelou said, "Once you know better, you do better."

   You can look back through your own timeline and find this to be true. There was once a time when your only option for pooping was in a diaper. As you grew, you learned there was a different choice available to you. You quickly developed bladder and bowel control to exercise a different choice – using the toilet. You traded in crawling for walking as soon as you discovered balance. You likely prefer a glass or a cup over a baby bottle these days and so on. As soon as your options open up, your decisions become better for you.

   The important thing to understand with this presupposition is that when a decision is made (or a behavior app is downloaded along the journey of life), it is the best choice available at the time. The behavior app becomes problematic when it keeps running in the background even after the usefulness is gone.

   Back in the days of the traveling circus, elephants were often tied to posts that weren't really strong enough to actually hold them. The elephants didn't escape because in their youth they had been chained to something that was strong enough to prevent them from wandering away. They learned quickly that the resistance on the chain prevented them from going anywhere so they simply stopped fighting it. Elephants grow up to be very big and very strong, but the post needs only be strong enough to put up a little initial resistance and the elephant will stop trying. Elephants are known for their memory, but it's not necessarily a favorable association, apparently.

You are not an elephant, but humans often behave in the same illogical way. It's like chewing on an old piece of gum long after it's lost its flavor and sometimes even after the jaw is sore from the chewing!

Our job is to help bring the limiting belief into awareness and then facilitate the exploration of options. Once the options are available, the client will naturally make different/better choices.

6. **Every behavior is useful in some context.**

Smoking cessation clients tend to have one thing in common: they started smoking to fit in, look older, be cool, join a group, etc. I've yet to talk with someone who started smoking because of a totally logical decision made entirely on the basis that they enjoyed the taste and the feeling of putting smoke in their lungs. (Because, in fact, they wouldn't even know what the feeling and taste was until they tried it!) And when their body resisted (because it's NOT NATURAL to smoke), they patiently trained themselves to smoke comfortably because the "reward" was bigger than the uncomfortable learning.

As a baby, flailing arms and legs coupled with screaming at thc top of one's lungs paid off in many ways when it was our only means of communication. We likely were turned over, fed, changed, cuddled, cooed, talked to, etc. Attention is a huge payoff. And later, when advanced communication skills didn't do the trick, uncontrolled anger might have been the behavior that continued to work to get a candy bar at the grocery checkout, a toy from an older sibling, or a night of comfort in Mom and Dad's bed. The SCM is the driver of behavior; it wants satisfaction. And one will continue to use the behavior until something more successful or more efficient comes along.

Serial killer John Gacy is a blight on Chicago's history. He killed thirty-three young men and buried them in the crawl space of his suburban home. It's an ugly story, and perhaps the most outrageous example I can use. But, I use it because we likely think anyone who could do such a thing must be "crazy." John Gacy was found to be completely sane. He was tried and later given a lethal injection.

Gacy was deemed sane because his actions were quite calculated. Years earlier in another state, two young men reported Gacy's advances to police and that resulted in some jail time for Gacy. He then moved to Chicago and in order to avoid being jailed again, he believed he had only one choice to preserve his freedom - summarily destroy the evidence that he had been with young men.

I covered this story back in my past life as a radio personality. In fact, that story started to unfurl just after I arrived in Chicago as a news announcer. I use this outrageous example of a "useful" behavior because I wonder if Gacy had been allowed and encouraged to exercise his same-sex interests in a non-judgmental way, would the murderous behavior have no longer been necessary? No way to know, I just wonder.

A behavior lasts until something more efficient or satisfying comes along to take its place. So, shake off that horrendous behavior story and realize every behavior has a positive intent and is useful in some context. Find what the behavior is doing FOR a person and you open their options for a change.

7. **The map is not the territory.**

People respond to their view of reality and not to reality itself.

We see examples of this all the time. Weight release clients sometimes say they decided to try hypnosis because they saw a picture of themselves (or caught a glimpse walking by a window) and "couldn't believe how big they'd become." They weren't living their life dealing with the reality of the size they'd created, they were dealing with the reality they had swirling around in their own mind and were shocked when confronted with actual reality.

Interestingly, that concept became quite useful for one weight release client who wanted to be a size 8. We explored what would be different when Kimmy was that size. I wondered if she could pretend to be a size 8 right there in the office. Kimmy imagined what she would wear, how she would stand, her facial expressions, her actions, the way she would eat, etc. And since she was so good at pretending to be a size 8 in the office, I wondered what might happen if she "really pretended" to be a size 8 for the rest of the day. Kimmy agreed to do it. When she returned a week later ("three pounds lighter without trying"), Kimmy shared that she loved being a size 8 so much, she pretended it every single day since our last session. She said that as she left the office the week before, she flirted with a man on the elevator and he flirted back! Kimmy reported standing taller, laughing louder, and said she ate much differently than she had before quite naturally, because a size 8 certainly wouldn't eat the way she had been eating! Her reality changed and her map was already changed in her mind. Belief is a powerful thing.

To build rapport, you first have to meet the client where they are. Be curious about the way they experience things. Forget about reality and discover how they've drawn the map and then be curious how they did that!

People are all unique. Check the cell phones of any two people and you'll find they manage their phones and apps in totally different ways. You wouldn't take their phone and start rearranging things, would you? So, you don't get to just step in and rearrange the way your client has their mind laid out. But you can be curious about the layout they have now and how things might be different if the arrangement was changed slightly.

When the client changes the arrangement, their map of the territory naturally makes a slightly different relief image.

8. **There is a solution to every problem. Experience has structure and anything can be accomplished if broken down into small enough pieces.**

   How do you eat an elephant? One bite at a time.

   How do you solve a problem? Specify!

   When a problem or limiting belief is chunked down into small enough parts, possibilities open. In the spring of 2021, I started working with a weight release client, Matt, who said he hadn't left his house since the beginning of the COVID pandemic and also sheepishly said he hadn't exercised much in the year before that either. When he started the program, his trips for groceries had been replaced by InstaCart and Matt had no idea of how to get motivated to exercise.

Since the pandemic was still a concern, Matt had no intention of going to a gym or hiring a personal trainer. Yet, he still needed help to get moving. I was curious about what he did while brushing his teeth. Matt said, "I just stand there and brush." I wondered if he'd be willing to march in place while he brushed his teeth, after all, he wasn't doing anything else with his feet and legs at that time. Matt smiled, shrugged his shoulders, and said, "Sure, I can do that!" I asked if he brushed his teeth in the morning and evening and he said, "Yes, and I have a Sonic Care brush that lasts for 2 minutes. So, I guess I'll be getting a 2-minute workout." I pointed out that we just doubled the time because twice a day means a 4-minute workout without breaking a sweat.

I could see belief written all over his face. So, I wondered where else he might be able to march in place while doing something else. He added marching movement while waiting for the Keurig to brew his coffee and at the refrigerator door while filling his water bottle. And he agreed to look for even more opportunities to do short bursts of movement throughout his day.

Another client purchased a Fitbit and spent a week living life as she always did in order to get a baseline of steps taken each day. After that first week, Anna looked forward to the challenge of adding 500 additional steps every day for a week, and then adding another 500 and another until she reached 10,000 steps a day. Anna's a client who likes a challenge and a winnable challenge set her in a new direction toward success.

Overwhelm can easily hijack the neocortex or the executive functioning/decision-making part of the brain. Chunking down can help naturally dissolve limiting beliefs and it's as if they were never there in the first place. (Soon, you'll be using the upcoming "magic questions" to give structure to easily moving the mindset from overwhelm to possibilities.)

9. **Each person is unique but one thing all have in common is each person already has most of the resources they need for a change.**

How could you desire something you know absolutely nothing about? It's hard to imagine without some frame of reference, is it not? So, when a client seeks an attribute, such as confidence, you can be reasonably sure they have an idea of what that means. And in that case, since we know that people have the resources they need, we can simply say, "Tell me about a time in your life when you experienced confidence." We can deepen their confidence trance by asking for specifics about what they're doing, who else is there, how do they know they are confident, how are they breathing, what's the look on their face, and what did they do then to reach THAT level of confidence. And we'll discover a strategy they've already used to get what they want now.

This pre-supposition helped remove my own overwhelm about being the "wizard." I no longer have to have all the answers for every person and every problem. My job has become the investigator who helps my client discover the resources they already have and can use. It's a lovely dance of discovering what steps the client already knows and then utilizing the feedback to facilitate a belief in new or different possibilities.

You know what Henry Ford said: "If you believe you can or if you believe you can't, you're right." So, why not discover what they believe they CAN do.

Before you get too carried away about your experience with a client who had no inner resources for her desire, realize that it's a dance! So, take the feedback and pivot; borrow the benefit from someone else. Remember, in order to ask for something, the client must have an example of that behavior in mind. They can model someone who has what they want and discover what steps that person takes to get there. It's pretty rare for someone to start out an expert. But as they follow another's STEPS TO SUCCESS, they can borrow the pattern and apply it to their own desire.

**10. People aren't broken, so they don't need fixing.**

I may have saved the most revelatory presupposition for last. It is not your job to fix people! They are working perfectly according to the way they're tending the programs.

Back to that cell phone analogy. One time in the Apple Store as I was buying a new phone, the Genius Bar was more than willing to transfer the data from my old phone to the new one, no problem. I handed my phone to the genius millennial and immediately got a look and an eyeroll. The expert cocked her head and said, "You have nine pages of apps! You know you can put those in folders, right?"

She didn't start rearranging my phone, but she did ask if I used all of those apps. I admitted I didn't even know why most of them were there anymore. And with another eye roll she explained that the apps not only take up space, but they can use battery strength just by running in the background. She offered to set up an iPhone introductory session so I could get help in arranging my phone. I smiled at the realization that a new metaphor for how the mind works had just been born!

Realize, that the phone, the mind or the body doesn't get overloaded accidentally.

If a person lives on a diet of junk food, candy and soft drinks and spends their time sitting and playing computer games, it is easy to understand how their body might be ballooning out of their jeans. But that's not because the person is broken. In fact, being overweight is a clear indication that the body is working exactly as it is being programmed to work.

So, cue Billy Joel for this dance: "Don't go changin'" anyone until you meet them where they are first! Be with them just the way they are, and be intently curious about how they're running the programs that they have now. Your curiosity will pay off as possibilities are revealed by the client. They will then begin a journey toward things they CAN do to affect a change.

This presupposition will bring you great dance partners time after time.

It is said that if you want someone to go into a trance, then you go first. Put this framework around the client, and see them as successful in reaching their goal. Then you will find that you do less "busy work around the client" and more inquisitive work with the client and have more successful sessions.

Quite a beautiful dance indeed.

CHAPTER 5:

# THE META PATTERN 4-STEP

You will, no doubt, recognize this pattern in many forms of persuasive speech. You'll notice it in commercials, TED Talks, political rhetoric, parental lectures, church sermons, etc., and, yes, in well-done hypnotic change work, eyes closed or wide open.

The Meta Pattern of Change takes one from a problem state to a solution state in four simple steps that facilitate a mindset shift.

> *Have you been stuck in the same job since graduation? Are you tired of sitting on the sidelines while your co-workers continue to advance around you? Is it harder and harder each month to stretch your money to pay the bills?*
>
> *Jump out of the slow lane and into the fast track toward a better life.*
>
> *Imagine relaxing into a career flexible enough to do it full or part-time from home. Imagine being your own boss...setting your own hours and your own salary. And imagine having all the new skills you need in just four short months.*

*Register now to become a Certified Hypnotist. Discover the skills to help yourself and help others manifest a better a life.*

That's a simple example of a hard sell using the 4-step Meta Pattern of Change.

- Associate into the problem state
- Dissociate from the problem state
- Associate into a resource state
- Paste the solution onto the problem for a change

Let's peek at a client who scheduled a session to work on procrastination. It wasn't a complete surprise when Fran walked into the office a bit late complaining about her current stress from the heavy traffic. Putting off discussing the problem at hand, Fran launched into a story about the inconsiderate driver who cut her off on the expressway.

Fran was already completely associated into that stress trance and it was getting in the way of the work she was in the office to do. So, I said, "Yes! Traffic is stressful! But, if it wasn't today...if it was any other day of the week, what day would you want it to be?"

Fran stopped, looked puzzled for just a moment and then exhaled as she said, "Saturday."

I smiled, nodded and said, "Yes, what makes Saturday a better day?"

She dreamily started talking about having no responsibility, no deadlines, a day when she doesn't even have to think because it's so easy and calming.

"That's right! And isn't that a nice thing to feel right now?"

Fran had walked into the office in a problem state. I broke that state by asking a really goofy question about a different day of the week.

I could have asked about anything other than stress or traffic and as soon as she accepted the suggestion to think about something else, we moved easily into what Fran wanted other than the stress she had been feeling at the time. And that cleared the way for us to talk about what procrastination was doing for her.

She gave me a wonderful launching point as I wondered if Fran noticed that she'd focused on a stress mindset to put off talking about procrastination. And I was curious about what else that behavior was doing FOR her. Remember there is always a positive intention behind every behavior.

Several years ago, I recognized my own procrastination gave me the adrenaline high that put me into quick action. And it served me quite well throughout my radio career because the entire show (my favorite part of every day) was an adrenaline rush to meet the deadlines. I enjoyed the self-made high.

The behavior was an asset in the well-staffed radio environment. It is helpful now during client appointments as I'm working against a "session deadline" or in speaking engagements working against getting it all said in the allotted time, etc., but the behavior was problematic at times in other endeavors because I waited for the "rush" to really get down to business. And that leads to a stress response when the paper jams in the hours just before notes or handouts need to be printed.

Creativity and flexibility aid in finding solutions. Once I understood what the behavior was doing FOR me, I was able to find other ways to get the rush without the stress. I no longer designate "flight time" as my deadline for being ready for a hypnosis conference. I set the deadline several days before an event now. (Not coincidentally, when I scheduled two days of downtime after a conference, I stopped having migraine headaches after returning from every event. I am now able to completely and happily relax and recharge my batteries without the need for the debilitating headache.)

I found the solution. I had to learn to cut myself some slack. To schedule downtime in my calendar and honor it. Plus, I gave up perfectionism. I'm not perfect at that yet, but I'm getting better all the time!

My problem with procrastination was solved by renaming it "pressure prompted."

I'm writing this book now (which has no particular "deadline") by using the Hemingway strategy. On a visit to Key West one year, a docent in the Hemingway House mentioned that the great writer was also quite an alcoholic and famous for his mile-long walk to his favorite bar every day. She said Hemingway had to find a way to keep himself out of the bar all day, so he made it a goal to write two thousand words before he allowed himself to leave his house.

Fascinating self-leverage, and the strategy must have worked because Hemingway was a prolific writer. I'm certainly no Hemingway, but I tried holding myself to two thousand words a day on this book until completion – and that was about to make me start drinking! So, I've found it quite successful to expect 1,000 words per day instead. See how well I'm doing with shunning perfectionism and adopting flexibility?! (I'm currently at around eight thousand words and it's coming easily.) It's difficult to solve a problem from the same mindset that created the problem. The Meta Pattern is a structure for changing the mindset.

When working with a client, as they talk about the problem, they associate into it and the dance is underway. It is the story (their personal B.S. Belief System) the client has been telling themselves to perpetuate the trance. And it is your first step in discovery about where they are now. I am usually curious about a "specific" time (maybe the most recent time) this issue was triggered. The more they talk about the issue, the deeper they go into the problem state, until you break that state with anything that sends the neural pathways moving in a different direction.

Once associated into the problem, it's time to change the dance step so we can move on to finding solutions. Realize, you don't have to listen to the whole “woe-is-me” story. As soon as the CLIENT is associated into their problem state, stop that story! Do not become hypnotized by the client’s B. S. Observe so you can discover what needs to change to make a difference.

Feel free to use any technique you choose to break the problematic trance state. When working with a client, I prefer a simple abrupt change of subject. I’ll say, “I ask a lot of weird questions, so just go with me on this. What was your first boyfriend’s/girlfriend’s name? Do you remember the color of their hair? How about their eyes?” The “change of topic” question isn’t really important. Remember, when what you’re doing isn’t working, try anything else. Well, in this case, the problem thinking isn’t working, so we move the subject to anything else.

- What would you rather feel instead?
- Where did you go on your last vacation?
- What’s your favorite color? What do you own that’s that color?
- Who was your third-grade teacher? What do you remember most about them?

While these types of questions change the state, you can also learn a lot about your client’s values as they talk. A transcript of a demo Outcome Specification “exploration” is ahead. You’ll discover the wonderful chunks of information that can be gleaned from curiosity about how the client believes what they believe.

Now that your client has switched out of the problem state, it’s time to go looking for solutions.

> When a client, Joan, needed the confidence to “speak like a pro” in her new leadership position with her company, I wondered when Joan would need that skill “specifically.” Joan said she would have to speak up in planning meetings and she would have to represent her department in quarterly

company-wide progress meetings.

I wondered if she'd ever felt genuine confidence before (knowing she must have or she couldn't be asking for it now). Joan spontaneously regressed to her teen years as an equestrian. She spoke proudly about winning trophies for hurdle jumping and I asked what she did to accumulate all that confidence. Joan said she loved what she was doing and she loved her horse. She said they practiced every day and developed a shared trust. Joan said by the time they arrived at a competition, they had it down to muscle memory and could just enjoy performing.

I wondered if there was any place in her future where she could use that same strategy of working so closely with her team that there is mutual trust and desire for success, a time when she might practice her speeches every day and get it into muscle memory so that she can just enjoy performing as she shares her success with a smile.

Joan smiled as she mapped across to using that "familiar" strategy in her new position. After all, she loves what she's doing, she works well with her colleagues and they all seem to support her leadership, and she will be thrilled to share that with the rest of the company at those quarterly "competitions."

That's the Meta Pattern in its simplest form. The change was made right there in conversation, in a few minutes, complete with resourceful regression!

Simply running through the Meta Pattern gave us what was needed for a change. And now, the client's conscious mind knows what to do. But remember, the conscious mind also hired me for hypnosis and this didn't "SEEM" like hypnosis. I don't want that part of the mind that is always looking for meaning and for reasons to begin to wonder how it could have been that easy. I now know what skills my client already has, what steps they will take in the future and the dance has just been choreographed for the “formal hypnosis” to reinforce the discoveries.

Do you now see how easily you can glide across the dance floor with your partner clients?

CHAPTER 6:

# ROCKIN' STEP BALL CHANGE

One of the first steps a beginning dancer might learn is the step-ball-change. And while it may look and feel a bit awkward at first, after just a few minutes, the new dancer can pick up speed and grace and elegance. You will find that to be true of the Meta Pattern and the upcoming "magic questions." You'll see a transcript of a demo session and how it fits together for a cohesive hypnosis process or script. And I'll add a few more helpful hints to keep in mind for investigation complete with a handy "check sheet" for use in subsequent sessions.

In a step-ball-change dance move, one puts weight on, say, the left foot, then shifts the weight and steps back on the right foot, and then rocks forward to the left foot. Shifting weight and stepping back on one foot gives leverage to rock forward to the original foot.

In change work, without leverage, there is no need to change. So, you'll watch and listen carefully for the motivation/leverage for change.

My dear friend (and brilliant change-master), Shawn Carson, offers this excellent explanation for the need to have leverage.

*Yes, leverage is required for change. The only exception is a pencil balanced on its point which will fall without leverage.*

*Rocks lying on a flat surface have no leverage (and don't change within measurable timescales).*

*Human beings are programmed for two things, stability and change. This allows us to stick with what works, and change what doesn't.*

*Your client's problem often arises because the stability program prevents them from making the change they need to make (note that this is not always the case, for example a serial philanderer has the opposite problem).*

*So you need leverage to overcome the stability of the problem to help (most of) your clients change.*

*What is leverage? It's the action of a lever, from levis meaning "light" (in weight). The lever allows you to move disproportionate weight by multiplying your strength.*

*Now you talk about "the leverage (is) whatever is holding the pencil on point." That's only partially true. There are two dynamics that hold the pencil on point; one is an "away-from" value, such as fear of change, the other is a belief such as "I can't change." Changing a belief, in this case to "I can change" is not "leverage" in my mind, because it doesn't have a multiplier effect. After all, I believe I can change, but if I don't desire to be different, or need to change, I won't.*

*So leverage is about the "desire" and "need." It's about the mother who lifts the car because her child is trapped underneath. It multiplies her strength.*

*So, what is this leverage? It's a value, and a value is a positive or negative emotion associated with an abstraction, in this case love. The mother loves her child and moves the car because she wants her child to be safe, or because she doesn't want her child to be harmed. In practice, both.*

*If your client doesn't have a positive value to move toward, and/or a negative value to move away from, they have absolutely no reason to change. You wouldn't even scratch your ass unless you have an itch and/or a desire to be comfortably itch free.*

*It's part of your job to ask "Why do you want to change? What's stopping you? How will you be as a person when this is no longer an issue for you?" Once you have their values, you leverage them for change.*

*"This is everything you'll have and be when you've made this change." If you want to use the away-from leverage: "This is the schmuck you'll remain if you don't." Use both, and you have Bandler's "propulsion system."*

***— Shawn Carson, www.TheIntelligentHypnotist.com***

Told ya he's smart!

Some clients will quickly tell you about their decision to change and why it's important now. But for some, it takes a few more steps,. Your flexibility to help clients discover their best steps leads to their empowerment.

Carl, a smoking cessation client, said he decided to change now because he'd just had his 56th birthday and it reminded him that his father died from lung cancer just before his 66th birthday. Carl said he was afraid if he didn't stop smoking now, he would die just like his father did. That's some pretty strong leverage.

I used a simple fork-in-the road metaphor. In that hyper-focused state of "formal hypnosis," Carl found himself at a point of decision, a fork in the road.

*I suggested that before he really makes up his mind, we try out the two roads. The one on the left is an easy, downward sloping road of least resistance...no change. It's just the "same ole-same ole" on through life.*

*The other road on the right is a little more uphill, but it's the right road to success. It's the road to change.*

*So, let's go down that low road on the left...no change at all. Down to the 1-year point of no change...look around...how's your cough now? Those burn holes in your shirt getting worse? (His list of reasons to quit) There's a mirror there, look in and notice...do you look smarter? Do you feel better?*

*Let's go down to the 5-year point of no change at all...look in the mirror....(repeat)*

*Let's go to the 10-year point...Oh, wait, before we go there, I'm going to have to ask you to look in the mirror to find out if you made it...that's 10 years, you'll be 66. Look in the mirror...did you make it?*

*Tears streamed down his face....*

*Let's not stay there...let's come all the way back up to the fork in the road. None of that has happened to you yet...and it doesn't have to.*

*Let's go up that road to success on the right...*

*It's 1-year smoke free! Notice how easy it was to walk up that hill...you look back down and realize that was just something you used to do...it's not a part of you anymore. Look in the mirror...is that a new shirt?*

*Let's go to the 5-year point...(repeat)*

*Let's go all the way up to the 10-year point. 10-years smoke-free! And look into that mirror there...what do you see? Do you look smarter? Do you feel better?*

*Carl got a big smile...a laugh...and some tears!*

*I wish I could leave you there in that happy time...but I can't. We have to go all the way back to that fork in the road.*

*And now...it's time to make that decision for yourself. I don't know what you'll decide. I don't know if you'll take that low road ...or if you'll take that right road to feeling better, looking better...I don't know what you'll decide today...But I'm confident you will make the <u>right</u> decision for you.*

When Carl emerged from the hypnosis session, he laughed and told me he was at his 66th birthday party and everyone was there. He said even his ex-wife showed up to celebrate his life!

That's what leverage can do for you. Pretty rockin', don't you think?

CHAPTER 7:

# HOW DOES YOUR CLIENT DANCE?

You don't need to know everything about your client to help them glide into the Trance Dance, but here are some things to discover. Knowing some or all of these about the client will help you form the suggestions and the "script" for change.

**Directly or Indirectly Suggestible?**

As you're building rapport, you can discover if your client is the kind of person who follows rules and likes to be told what to do or if they're the kind of person who wants options so they can make up their own mind.

A trick I learned from the world of Stage Hypnosis often gives me clues about an in-office client's suggestibility. Upon entering my office, there are a variety of places a client might sit. There are two straight-backed "lobby" chairs, a desk chair, a chair at a table and a recliner. I enjoy watching the first choice made by a client. Some walk in and stand just inside the door waiting until I tell them where to sit (directly suggestible). Some clients walk straight to the recliner and start to sit down before I stop them (inferred or indirect as they're making their own decisions about the way reality should go). I stop them simply to begin gently instructing that in my office, they follow my suggestions. And then I have them sit at the table and fill out some paperwork. It's just as interesting to watch what happens on a second visit. Often, even the indirectly suggestible client will wait to find out where to sit for this appointment. All the while, I am observing and collecting data about how the client maps their reality so I can capitalize on the strengths they already possess.

Whether the client is directly or indirectly suggestible may depend on the specific situation. And it's a good example of why there is no "one-size-fits-all" weight loss program that is 100% effective. Totally independent thinkers may be completely flummoxed by food and may do much better with a diet plan that tells them what to eat and when to eat. Others find the rigors of a diet are intolerable and they may do better with modifications such as '"eat 10% less of everything" which keeps their options open but reduces portion size.

One "options" client, Peggy, loved the idea of UK hypnotist Paul McKenna's four simple rules: 1. When you're hungry, eat. 2. Eat what you want, not what you should. 3. Eat slowly and consciously. 4. When you think you're full, stop. Peggy repeated the four rules, laughed and said it would be so easy.

On her second visit, Peggy said mealtime was now fraught with panic. "Since I have to eat what I WANT, not what I should, I have no idea what I WANT sometimes and so I can't figure out what to eat." Peggy fared much better when I quizzed her about what rules might work for her. She decided to pick from a variety of low-carb options at mealtimes and then choose the ones she wants at that meal. With that problem solved, Peggy enjoyed practicing the rest of the McKenna guidelines. The dance of flexibility allowed her to have her rules...and eat them too.

**Toward or Away:**

Be on the lookout for hints of motivational styles. Is the client moving away from pain or heading toward pleasure/a goal?

In the transcript of the Outcome Specification coming up, Janet clearly shows she utilizes an “away from” strategy when she says she wants to eliminate (get away from) self-doubt. It takes a little bit of tap dancing to get Janet to focus toward what she wants which, she says, is confidence so she can increase her client base and make more money.

The client who says they “want to be a size 8!” is clearly moving toward something.

Another of my weight release clients, Ed, said, “I just don’t want my knees to hurt so much anymore.” That’s an “away from” strategy. Remember, I don’t give advice, although I do persuade, so my follow-up dance move was, “A cardiologist once told me something compelling about knees. He said every pound of weight is like four pounds of pressure on your knees. Every ten pounds you release is like taking FORTY pounds of pressure off of your knees. So, how much would you need to release to feel better?” Ed said twenty pounds would likely make a big difference. And now suddenly we’re heading toward a goal.

That change of direction was expedited by quoting an expert. That expert opinion gave Ed something tangible to imagine and calculate a solution that was believable and consequently achievable. And that, in turn, becomes the outcome we work toward and the suggestion I repeat as we go forward with his eyes open or closed.

**Internal or External:**
In the demonstration transcripts coming up, Janet shows her external locus of control when she mentions she liked her first boyfriend because “he liked her.” And her self-proclaimed “comparison anxiety” is likely because she’s waiting for others to tell her she’s “enough.” This is a clue that ego-strengthening techniques may be of benefit.

Dee, on the other hand, in the Personal Trance Words transcript coming up, clearly is self-directed. She says the way she knows she's done a good job at something is personal satisfaction. Dee is inwardly motivated. I would help her build in HER benchmarks of achievement and suggest she note them in her journal as she writes her story of success. Realize, I didn't make up that suggestion, you'll see how easy that one is to make. When you get to that transcript, recognize this stuff just writes itself when you patter using their leverage and their goal.

**Global or Specific:**

Does your client see the big picture first and then work back to the details? Or does your client organize their mind with details first working out to the destination?

I listen for the covert globalization excuse. "You know, you can't walk past an open candy dish without taking something!" I tend to respond to an excuse such as this with a shocked expression, "What are you talking about? I never take anything from a candy dish. I don't like candy!"

The client was allowing their candy-snacking issue to become ubiquitous. "YOU can't pass a candy dish..." takes it out of personal control because, in their B.S., the problem belongs to everyone. Have your client own it. When they say, "I can't pass a candy dish without taking something," they automatically reclaim their control and can choose to make a different decision about that dreaded dish and its contents.

So, I hold my fingers out in a dramatic cross when I confront that belief. It's a bit of a shock to the client and stops that old thinking right in its tracks. Then I suggest that my client take back their power by repeating, "I can't pass a candy dish without taking something." Personal power is restored automatically as they realize they can make any decision about that candy dish that they want to. They may CHOOSE to take a piece, or they can just as easily choose to negatively hallucinate the candy in the dish (not even give it any attention) and walk on by. They might decide to take a different route to their desk. They could even ask the receptionist for help by moving the dish out of sight. I'm not saying all of those ideas are necessary, I'm simply suggesting that owning one's response to the candy opens up a wealth of options for alternate actions. And that's when words have internal power to make an easy change.

This category can also indicate what's most important to the client. Is it the big picture or the detail? Neither is preferable, but it's nice to know how the client views the world.

During my radio career, it never really interested me how it was possible for someone across the country to hear my voice. I just knew that they could and that was cool! The big picture was good enough for me. Even today, I couldn't care less about how Zoom works. I just know it does and I know how to access the virtual filters to add lipstick! My husband, on the other hand, is a television technical manager. His detail-orientation is the perfect skill for his gig. And at home, our two styles make for a good partnership.

For good communication, it helps us when we're mindful of the other's natural style. When navigating on a car trip, I like my directions something like this: We're going to St. Louis, via I-57, in 5-miles you will merge to the right.

My husband prefers it in reverse. We'll merge right in 5-miles to take I-57 to St. Louis. Neither is right or wrong. But utilizing the natural preference of the other reduces travel stress a full notch. And it's well worth the effort.

You may find yourself using the client's strategy or guide them to explore something different.

**Once or Several Times:**
When making decisions, do you see it and get it? Or would you prefer to do research and see several different varieties then make comparisons before buying?

This is handy information in sales. You can apply the knowledge to suggestions too. I have to honestly say I rarely intentionally go looking for this answer. But when it comes up, I let it play into the patter of the trance.

A person who makes snap decisions may grow restless at the repetition of identical suggestions, sometimes called "direct drive" suggestions. For this client, change up the wording or offer stories or metaphors that allow the client to map across to the application. Meanwhile, a person who has to "sleep on it" or needs to think about it for a while, might benefit from repeated suggestions along with the direction to listen to a recording for a period of time to "seal" the suggestion.

Advertisers live by repetition which is why you continue to see and hear McDonald's ads on television and radio. Even that iconic brand has to stay top-of-mind aware or it could simply fade away...forgotten. (Just like a suggestion for some clients.)

Repetition is one way to affect a change. When one sees, hears, or does something enough times, it becomes automatic. And this is one reason to give your client something to listen to for a series of days or weeks or months. In my large Hypno Center, we practiced repetition. And it was interesting to note, when the client "bought in" to listening to hypnosis recordings twice a day every day (to think themselves thin!), they made other changes progressing to their goals. We also noticed that the clients who gave up the habit of listening often also gave up the habit of changing. (Energy flows where attention goes.)

There are two reliable ways to make a change. Trauma or shock can produce instant change. A girlfriend of mine was well-known for racing through yellow traffic lights to "beat the red." And she did it every time, until that one day when the timing was just a little off and her car was totaled. She was unhurt but the shock/trauma changed her relationship with yellow lights instantly. She slows and stops for them now.

Some hypnotists use a "shock" induction to move their client from consciousness to hypnosis. That's not generally my style to induce hypnosis, but responding to a client in an exaggerated "shocking" manner often opens the channels to slipping in a suggestion for something different.

A self-proclaimed procrastinator might say, "I'm always late for everything." And, I might animatedly say, "Really? If there was a million-dollar money-giveaway, I'll bet you would show up on time." When the client agrees, we've started the dance routine of chipping away at that old limiting belief. And now we can explore the times they do things on time and capture some info on what needs to change to make a difference here.

So, it can be fun to recognize whether your client will benefit from repetition or can have a lightbulb moment and change for good.

**Independent or Team Player:**
When you do get to the examples coming up, notice that Dee is going to take her decision and run with it and make it work. (At least that's what we "know" with the limited info-gathering in this demo.)

With Janet, I utilize a younger version of herself as an accountability partner. Janet indicates that she performs reliably when someone is counting on her and holding her to her promises. So, why not make that readily available.

You may become the accountability partner for your client. When I work with weight release clients, I want a relatively long commitment (depending on the amount of weight to be released). Then as incremental changes are made, they can count on me to cheer them on to the next level of achievement or to aid finding solutions for plateaus or frustrations. Weight release tends to carry many layers and I find it important to be there as things change and we deal with new aspects that are revealed.

I also provide recorded programs and/or books and videos as necessary. For those people who are more self-directed and like to do things on their own in their own time, recorded material or classes are available on my website. For a client who needs repetition, I can easily make a pre-recorded process available to them for repeated listening. There are many ways to facilitate a change and the prospective client has a right to choose the level of personal attention they prefer when learning something new.

**Communication Cues:**
Whether you've studied NLP or not, you've likely learned or heard something about VAK – Visual, Auditory and Kinesthetic representational systems. One of the leading NLP experts in the world, Michael Watson, explains it this way in his NLP Practitioner's Manual:

> *Remember that according to [Alfred] Korzybski, "the map is not the territory" and that we are all engaged in creating our own descriptions or "maps" of the worlds and the meaning of things, and the relationships between things, etc. We represent the world to ourselves in the form of sensory data. We experience and create images and sounds/words, feelings, tastes and smells. It is suggested that we don't interact with the world directly or reality per se, but with these representations. Experience, therefore, is a creative act.*
>
> *Since people are experiencing the world through their representations, it can be useful to know which representational systems are being used consciously and which are outside of awareness.*
>
> *Through trained attention and sensory acuity, you can develop clues as to the thinking processes of another person...and your ability to respond to these clues can have a tremendous impact on your effectiveness as a communicator.*
>
> **— Michael Watson www.Phoenix-Services.org**

When one is unsure of a client's representational system, it's easy enough to say something like, "...maybe you'll see it...maybe you'll feel it...maybe you'll hear it...or maybe you'll just pretend, whichever way you prefer is just fine." But imagine the fluidity of the dance when you are in step with your client's preferred system.

If your client is primarily visual, they may talk about "looking" into their future or "seeing" their "bright" future or "visualizing" all of their problems. You now have a clue about their internal representational system.

Your client might say "I hear you" or "that sounds right to me" or it "rings a bell." They're giving you information about the importance of their auditory preference.

And you may have a client who "feels your pain" or who wants to get a "handle" on something or they may say, "it just makes my skin crawl"; all good indicators of a kinesthetic bent.

Realize, we all use all of our senses at all times, but some people definitely have a preferred system. If they're quite kinesthetic, you can certainly teach them how to be more visual, but you've got to wonder about the efficacy. If the client can get the change they want using the representational system that they prefer, why not cut to the chase and use all the information you gather overtly or covertly to assist the progress of the session. And make a note of it so that you can use it again for subsequent sessions.

V-A-K are the most common systems. But, after all, we do have five senses so it would be unfair to leave out olfactory, as in the sweet "smell" of success, and gustatory, something leaves a bad "taste" in my mouth.

I've found it rare to have a client who uses these systems exclusively. However, I did have one amazingly gustatory tobacco chewer. Hank wanted to quit chewing tobacco. It was so "juicy" to listen to him talk about it. He mentioned how much he truly enjoys the "taste" of his "mint-flavored" chew. Hank talked about "gritting his teeth" when they made him work overtime. He told a story about getting frustrated when he couldn't remember the exact detail of something, but had it right on the "tip of his tongue." I had to stifle a giggle because it was as if he'd made a list of gustatory words to use before coming in for the session.

Interestingly, he was quite "tight-lipped" about "spitting out" any possible solutions and had a difficult time releasing that oral-based habit. When I asked him to "chew on" the idea of his young sons following in his footsteps, sneaking tobacco or vaping because "Daddy does it," we made some inroads. Along the way, Hank mentioned he's a country music fan and it reminded me of a country song I once heard about a dad and his little buckaroo who watched everything Dad did and wanted to grow up to be just like him. Hank knew the song ("Watching You" by Rodney Atkins) and teared up. Emotion and leverage! Yay! Suddenly, life "tasted a little sweeter" for Hank and he decided to download that song and listen to it on the way to and from work every day. Now that's some flexible use of repetition! And it's a solution that worked.

Knowing the client's preferred representational system didn't get us to the solution, but it did explain a bit about how he was so tied-in to this particular habit.

So, you can do a deep dive into NLP's eye accessing cues, gestures, etc. Or you can use your own common sense as you observe your client. In the upcoming transcripts you'll notice that Janet is easy. She makes use of all three primary representational systems quite fluently, visualizing, feeling, and hearing. Connecting with either one or all three is excellent.

Even though the upcoming transcript of eliciting Personal Trance Words is a short list, Dee clearly establishes her connection to kinesthetic suggestions. She "feels deep inside."

Remember, you don't have to gather ALL of this information. But the more you practice this, the easier it will be and the more information you will naturally take in.

For a handy tool, I've included the Hypnotist's Tracking Sheet at KarenHand.com/Trance-Dance that will allow you to easily take notes during your conversational intake and keep those tips for quick reference during subsequent sessions.

CHAPTER 8:

# THE OUTCOME OVERTURE

You can't get there unless you know where you're going. It doesn't matter if you're running errands, picking up the kids after school, or going on vacation, you can't get there without knowing the destination. And the same goes for the hypnotic journey. To lead it successfully to the desired conclusion, you've got to know the desired outcome. Then the rest begins to naturally fall in place.

Understand, for the clinical hypnotist, the outcome is whatever the client reasonably desires. In the real world, the outcome is whatever the persuader desires. So, suggestions aren't always to YOUR benefit, but persuasion is always designed to benefit a desired outcome.

A friend tells a story of running a clothing store in his youth that specialized in selling jeans. When Joe took over the business, sales were okay, but he wanted to make his mark and be a bigger success than his predecessor. Joe went into the dressing rooms in his store and put a book of matches under the top corners of the mirrors hanging on the walls. That gave a slight tilt to the mirror which magically made everyone look a little slimmer...just like in the funhouse at the fair! Sales went through the roof. Joe's desired outcome was realized! And now, as you look back, have you ever noticed that the clothes tried on in the store sometimes look way better than when you see them in your home mirror, mirror on the wall? Many fine clothing stores tilt their mirrors slightly. So, realize, not all suggestions you hear (or see) are necessarily beneficial to you but they do lead to a desired outcome.

The intended outcome is always the place to start in suggested change.

Taking a vacation is a pleasant example to use. I've heard people say, "I need (or want) a vacation." But it isn't until they DECIDE to TAKE a vacation that plans are really underway. The moment you DECIDE, the plan starts to take shape. For the hypnosis client, the DECISION to change is made when they go looking for a hypnotist. They go deeper into that decision trance when they call, do a screening or consultation, and schedule the appointment.

Once the decision to take a vacation is made, you can begin to imagine the possibilities of your destination. For this example, let's take a tropical vacation on the island of Jamaica. We immediately know that we won't be driving or walking or taking a train, so we check flight schedules and find the perfect direct flight into Montego Bay. Each step gets easier and easier as our excitement grows.

Our outcome is to get some relaxing beach time and some fun activities over our 7-day stay. We find a nice all-inclusive resort just outside of town. It will be convenient for a day trip into Montego Bay and for another day trip to Ocho Rios to play in the falls, so we're set. Now we can relax and begin to imagine more fun details about the trip. Our thoughts are now turned toward shopping for new swimwear, sundresses and sandals. We can pack light and this will be a great trip. Anticipation is building.

See how easy it is to put together the "details" of that trip? It's easy because we know the desired outcome and with the magic questions, you can discover some interesting tidbits along the way.

In a client session, those tidbits of knowledge make up the script on the journey to change.

My favorite structure for going from desire to script is based on the NLP Outcome Specification Exercise. I actually see it as an intervention. The questions drill down to what the client wants and exactly what it will take for them to get there. They'll tell you everything you need to know.

First, you'll see the questions which form the structure of the dance steps. The art of hypnosis is then applied as the artist weaves curiosity in and around the questions to create the session success. After the questionnaire, you'll see a transcript of a session with notations on how each answer gives us clues about what to do to help the client.

Also realize, these questions are hypnotic because they SEEM to be simple conversation about the clients' favorite subject, themselves. But, the questions are also a covert fractionation technique. Each time you ask a question, the client goes inside their own mind to find the answer. They then "come back out to the present" to give you the answer. You ask another question, they go back in, etc., as you lead the dance of discovery.

**Outcome Specification Questions:**

1. ***What do you want? Or, what change do you want to make today?***

   Manage the response. You can use a **Smart Goals** model: **S**pecific, **M**easurable, **A**chievable, **R**elevant and **T**ime-bound, to help your client manage their own expectations. You're looking for small chunk size changes, controlled by the client and specific in nature that offers a measurement for accountability.

   An answer such as "I want to be happy" doesn't really give us much on which to work. Dig deeper. Find out what "happy" means to the client. Remember, it's just a code word. So be sure you clearly understand what the code means before proceeding. An answer of "I want to quit smoking" is a bit more specific. I still dig deeper to find out exactly how they want to do that. Do they want to go cold-turkey or taper off of cigarettes with a slow goodbye? I don't care either way. I just want to know how they want to do it so I can be specific in my suggestions for change and know that we're both going for the same outcome.

**What <u>specifically</u> will that do <u>for</u> you?**

Specificity is there for a reason. A response like "I'll feel better" is a little too vague. Better than what? What exactly does it mean to "feel better"? How much better do you want to feel, specifically?

You can find some leverage points here if you're willing to be curious. For example, a smoking cessation client says, "My wife wants me to quit." Well, first of all, don't take that client! That can lead to resentment and failure. Take the feedback and tell your prospective client to call you back when THEY are ready to quit smoking.

But if the client replies, "Then I'll get rid of this cough, and hopefully I can walk up a flight of stairs without having to stop and catch my breath," now you've got a little leverage with which to work.

You're looking for what the **client** will get out of making this change and what makes it worthwhile.

2. ***How will you know when you have it?***

Lots of good info available in this answer. Some may say, "I'll just know." Which is good because it may indicate an internal locus of control. But go farther anyway and ask for "evidence." You might probe deeper by saying, "Yes, you'll know! But how, exactly, will you know it?" (Remember, you want achievable measurements the client can notice along the way. Success breeds success!)

The client may indicate they'll know "when people start to notice." Again, good information because they're telling you they are externally focused. Then help them find some clues within themselves to gauge how well they're doing. Leaving it up to other people to notice is risky.

Keep being curious until the client comes up with a clue or two they can notice as signs of success. Then encourage them to go looking for even the tiniest indication of success. You want to help them go looking for what they WANT instead of what they DON'T want. When you know whether your client is moving TOWARD a goal or AWAY from pain, it helps design the strategy.

3. ***Where, when, and with whom do you want it?***

You're checking in to make sure they've thought it through and can begin to imagine how the change will look, sound, and feel in their life.

If a client were to say they want to be more aggressive, check it out. "With everyone? I mean, if a cop pulls you over, is aggression the behavior you want in that case?" And then encourage the client to ***specify*** exactly where, when and with whom this change will be a benefit.

Ask. And then listen! Be relentlessly curious! You'll find out what people believe about themselves and the world around them. You'll discover incredibly interesting ways that people organize their thinking. Curiosity may have killed the cat, but, it was satisfaction that brought him back!

4. ***How will this affect other aspects (or people) in your life?***

I've had weight release clients who say they always regain the weight as soon as they start receiving compliments, or their husband begins getting jealous, or when they get tired of any particular diet. That's an indication that external forces are going to play heavily on the success of this goal. Your client is also likely to need some help with ego strengthening, worthiness and tenacity.

This is the question that allows the client to begin trying on different solutions to any limitation that comes up. Plus, it helps you discover other aspects of the issue that your client may not have even realized until now.

Your client might instead say, "I want this everywhere and with everyone. And anyone who doesn't like it, well, they're wrong." Wow, sounds pretty self-directed, doesn't it? So, the answer to the next question will be interesting....

5. ***What stops you from having this already?***

You'll find the limiting beliefs that need to be changed here. Clients may say things such as, "It runs in my family." And you can begin to do the reframing work there.

One client, Tom, wanted exercise motivation and told me he just hates exercise. I asked for his definition of exercise. Tom said, "Moving your body for an hour...and sweating a lot." His face wrinkled up as he explained.

I told Tom I didn't blame him for hating that! And then I wondered if he'd heard about the latest research that shows short bursts of exercise may be even better than long sustained workouts. I was curious about whether or not Tom would do shorter pieces of movement, like marching in place while brushing his teeth or parking farther away from a store entrance or doing five jumping jacks after every phone call he completes. Tom didn't like the jumping-jacks idea, but said he could park farther away and take the stairs instead of the elevator one floor up to his office. And the change was already taking place.

I used "new research" as the leverage to break up his limiting belief about how awful exercise HAS to be and opened up a world of new opportunities for successful change. By the way, covertly, I also used the word movement to replace exercise and during the "formal hypnosis" added the post-hypnotic suggestion to find new and appealing ways every day to MOVE MORE.

Whatever has been stopping the client from getting what they want is likely a clear indication of where some change has to take place either right now in the discussion or later in subsequent sessions.

6. ***What resources do you already have that will help you obtain your outcome?***

These resources can be tangible such as a treadmill or time to practice a speech or they can be inner resources.

You probably remember the client I mentioned who wanted confidence and remembered how sure of herself she'd felt when she was a champion equestrian as a teenager. A quick trip back to that time let Joan see how she achieved confidence. She practiced every day and worked like a team with her horse. Joan knew each routine so well it was in muscle memory. When she went out to perform, all she had to do was enjoy the performance. We applied that solution to Joan's new work responsibilities of making more speeches (practicing the material, getting the words into muscle memory, enjoying the performance) and the resources she found inside made excellent suggestions to be used in the "formal hypnosis." Some resourceful regression and then future pacing layered with direct suggestions became the "script."

In this example, a little "mini regression" to Joan's resources was as easy as being even more curious. When I inquired about past experience with confidence (her resources), Joan shrugged a bit and offhandedly said, "Oh, when I competed in high school." The regression deepened when I said, "Tell me about that!" and I got a string of helpful suggestions for this current issue.

During the "formal hypnosis," we focused a bit more of her attention on everything Joan did before the competition to build her confidence. Joan "revivified" even more examples of working then to create that confidence and we future-paced those examples into her new job requirements and together we'd danced toward success.

7. ***What additional resources do you need to obtain it?*** *(Feel free to replace "it" with the SPECIFIC issue.)*

Extremely useful and practical ideas come up here all the time. One client, Amy, who wanted to do more daily writing, already had a computer and a bunch of ideas. In this follow-up question, she came up with moving her computer to the breakfast nook where she really enjoyed being surrounded by windows and feeling so close to nature. That was the change that made the difference for her. Amy discovered she was able to do a lot more writing and was happier while doing it just by moving her laptop to a better location. You see, finding even an easy solution is much harder when you're working from the problem mindset. But when one goes looking for solutions, they're likely to find them!

It reminds me of a story I read in Reader's Digest years ago about a woman at an AA meeting who received a token celebrating her accomplishment. She was asked about the times that are the most difficult for maintaining sobriety. (Now, that's a way of keeping someone associated into the problem!! But I digress....) She told the room that the only time it was hard for her was on an airplane. She traveled a lot for work and said when the drink cart came down the aisle, she ordered. But didn't drink it. She simply stated the hardest time for her was holding her vodka tonic while NOT drinking it. She said, "Sometimes my hands are literally shaking when they come back around to collect the full cup."

Someone asked why she continued to ask for her old nemesis, the Vodka Tonic. Surprisingly, the woman said she never even considered there was another option. She was stuck in the problem state. When it was suggested that she can ask for a soda or coffee or anything non-alcoholic, she breathed a sigh of relief, admitted it had never occurred to her to order something else and said she would use that solution the next time.

It's amazing what a mindset can do – for and against you. And equally amazing how effective a well-placed belief change can be to one's success. (It also shows one doesn't have to be a trained hypnotist to suggest something that sticks. But that's material for another book!)

In this phase of the questioning, your client has already been in and out of the solution trance a few times. No need to break rapport by giving advice here. Simply ask the question and take the feedback. If the client says there's nothing else needed, go with that! But, notice how many times they'll come up with something even better when you ask if they need additional resources.

***8. How are you going to get there?***

Let your client tell you their plan. They've moved from the problem state to the solution state by now so ideas usually flow fairly easily. And this is where the client will give you the plan for success.

***First step—Be specific and achievable.***

Usually, the clients are quite ready here to imagine a plan for success and design their own route for getting there. A client might say, "Well, first, I'm moving my laptop when I get home. The breakfast nook is surrounded by windows, so, before I begin to write, I'm going to notice how good it feels to be surrounded by so much beauty. I'll watch the trees sway in the breeze, the birds stop by the feeder and remind myself how natural it is for me to write. And then I'll just begin with whatever is on my mind to get the juices flowing."

*"And it feels so good to have a natural plan to write daily. Imagine your laptop in the breakfast nook...you're sitting there...the windows let in the light, you can notice the trees and the birds...and it feels so good to be surrounded by the beauty of nature, as you begin to write...about the beauty, or about anything else that's on your mind. You find the surroundings are so natural, that you automatically do what's so natural for you and you begin putting your thoughts on the page...with no judgement, just pure joy of writing...being in sync with nature. And take that wonderful feeling into your future. Notice how much easier it is to do your daily writing because it feels so good to be doing something so natural...so automatic...so easy and enjoyable for you..."*

It's easy to take your client's words and ideas and let them flow naturally toward the goal that is desired. And through this questionnaire, you will get many more ideas to incorporate. And you can easily bring in their benefits as well to deepen the trance and give leverage to the suggestions.

***Is there more than one way to get there?***

If you've gone down the list asking the questions in order, by this time, you've narrowed down the goal, it's measurable and achievable and you have a plan for success. So, why open this can of worms? Well, it doesn't hurt to have more than one option.

This can be a contingency plan or it can be what happens if something doesn't go as planned. If you can't walk a mile in the park because it's raining...what might you do instead?

Back to our vacation on Jamaica, if the resort we pick has no vacancy while we're there, well, there's always a trip across the island to the resorts and reggae in Negril.

Notice how the questions move through the Meta Pattern. First, one is associating into their problem/desired change, then moving toward solutions and the steps to get there.

If, along the way your client has difficulty moving out of the problem, you can break the problem state. Ask about anything else. I might go off on a tangent of other questions such as, "This might be a weird question, but do you remember your first date? Who did you go out with? Where did you go?" And then return to the outcome questions. While they were thinking about their first date (or car or school or whatever), they're no longer thinking about that issue. And they can move easily from that positive memory trance to a solution trance.

While you're breaking the problem state, listen carefully to their answers for the "off the topic" questions. You'll pick up a lot of "Personal Trance words" along the way that will help you deliver suggestions in the most understandable way for your client. You elicit values with personal trance questions. And we'll look at that in more depth shortly.

Realize, you can ask the outcome questions in order as they appear and the results will be effective. After you've practiced with these questions a few times, it will become quite conversational and natural. Leverage your own curiosity about your client to facilitate this exploration and relax! Recognize, you're getting the solutions from the client and you're placing the responsibility where it belongs—on the client who is the one who will have to do the work to make the change.

Resist the urge to work harder for your client's change than they work for it. But, if you do insist on holding on to the responsibility for your client's change, at least charge a price commensurate with following them around and keeping the cigarettes out of their mouth! Otherwise, facilitate a solution and send your client away empowered with a workable solution toward their goal.

I'm not suggesting a one-session wonder, although it does happen with a well-formed outcome on many issues, but, I am encouraging you to dance. In NLP studies, it's referred to as pacing and leading.

Remember, the Hypnotic Trance Dance is a combo step that starts by learning what the client already believes and discovering what they need to learn to create the successful outcome they've hired you to achieve. And also remember, they have to be able to do the steps placed in the routine. If they can't do the splits, don't put the splits into the dance! But if they have a skill already, why not use it to their full advantage!

My outcome for this intake process is two-fold: to gather information and to point the client's attention toward solutions. As long as you stay focused on getting just the information you need to facilitate the client's outcome, you can avoid being hypnotized by the client's story. Recognize, you have to maintain control of the "conversation" and remember the purpose isn't to have a friendly chat, but to efficiently gather information and make some noticeable progress for the client in the time allotted. Then you can map the strategy for going forward if more sessions are necessary to successfully complete the change.

Now that you've got an idea of what to look for, coming up next is a transcript from an Outcome Specification demonstration I did at the Virtual Mid-America Hypnosis Conference in 2020.

After reading the transcript, go to KarenHand.com/Trance-Dance and download a printable copy of the outcome questions and Hypnotist tracking sheet. Add a layer of learning by watching the video and making your own notes on the handouts.

CHAPTER 9:

# THE REHEARSAL – DEMO TRANSCRIPT

*K. Alright, Janet, what do you want? What change do you want to make right now?*

You're looking for a specific positive change.

*J. I wanna erase some* ***self-doubt*** *so that I can attract more clients to my hypnosis business or practice, or whatever I want to call it.*

Away from motivation

Leverage = more clients.

*K. So you want to erase self-doubt.* <u>*Tell me a little bit about that self-doubt.*</u>

Associating into the issue.

*J. I have a lot of...kind of like* ***comparison anxiety****. Cause I'll see my peers and they appear so successful and there are so many people that I admire who do this work. And many of them have done it a lot longer than I have, so I guess, there's*

A limiting belief to unravel.

| | |
|---|---|
| *really not a...good comparison. But I feel like, well, if they can do it, how come I'm not doing it. So, I kinda hold myself short as a result.* | |
| *K. I'm curious, (BTW, ya'all this isn't on the sheet, I'm branching off the sheet a little bit because I operate on curiosity.) I'm curious a little bit, as you're thinking those thoughts about that comparison anxiety, comparing yourself to others...are you telling that to yourself. Are you seeing that...* | People are fascinating! And I want to know specifically how they do it. |
| *J. Oh, I'm sure I'm telling it to myself, you know it's in that, "you're not good enough", kind of background noise.* | Now we know we have an audio track that may need attention. |
| *K. And is that your voice or someone else's voice?* | Let's get specific. |
| *J. That's a good question, I'm not real sure. I always thought it was my voice, but I had never really paid that close attention, I just know that it was negative.* | Such a bizarre question lends itself to an instant confusion induction. |
| *K. OK, I hear that it's a negative voice but would you mind giving it some thought. Go to a place where you've had this comparison anxiety at some point and just notice. It might be your voice...it might be somebody else's voice. I'm just curious.* | On the spot/instant regression. |

| | |
|---|---|
| *J. Wow! It's not my voice.* | (Told ya it was instant!) |
| *K. Oh, who's voice is it?* | Relentlessly looking for specifics. |
| *J. Well, there's probably several. It might be my mom or it might be my brother or sister.* | *Make a note, this may be worth exploring. |
| *K. OK. Just curious about that.  Isn't that an interesting thing to discover?* | We don't need any more on that right now. |
| *J. Yeah...* | |
| *K. We'll come back to that in a moment. So, who was your first boyfriend?* | Breaking the state of discovering voices. |
| *J. I...uh...let's see...I can remember his last name was P______. I can't remember his first name. Cause I was like in third grade* | She's in a different trance now. |
| *K. I was going to ask how old you were...third grade...was he the cutest boy in class? Why was it you liked P_______ so much?* | Deepening the association. |
| *J. Oh, he pursued me. He was persistent. I was so flattered, like "Oh my gosh,* ***somebody likes me****."* | Indicates external locus of control. Letting others determine her worth. |

*K. So he was persistent. Thank you very much for sharing that with me. I appreciate that.*

Unwanted (for now) audio associations broken.

*Let's go back to that comparison anxiety for just a moment. When you don't have this...what would you have?*

*J. I'd have full* ***confidence*** *and* ***pride****...those are the biggies.*

Benefits of change. Good personal trance words.

*K. And when you're confident and proud, what does that do for you?*

Looking for leverage to make the change.

*J. It keeps me* ***happy*** *and* ***open*** *cause* ***I love to share and teach****. You know, when I've learned something I've got to teach it to someone else immediately and usually it's something they already knew. But I didn't know that cause I'd just learned it. (Laugh) So, you know, I get more open and* ***giving****.*

Personal values to build up. Personal trance words in bold.

*K. So, what I heard you say is, as soon as you learn something new you want to teach it to somebody else. You want to share the wealth.*

*J. Exactly!*

*K. I'm right there with you man. As soon as I learned hypnosis I wanted everybody to know about it. I've got the coolest thing.*

Meeting her where she is and building rapport.

*J. This is so cool, you've got to find out about this. You've got to share it.*

Confirmation we're in sync.

*K. You can get yourself in trouble with that, Janet. I took my newfound confidence and knowledge...and my new business cards out to a bunch of smokers standing on the corner and walked up to them and said, "I've got this great thing and I can help you with that". I gave them my business cards and they...threw them in the garbage. Because that was before I understood that everyone is in a trance. They were in the smoking trance they weren't in the 'Let me get out of this' trance.*

"Personal story" to break up the limiting belief she mentioned.

Telling a story is an effective change technique in or out of deep trance.

*J. Yeah, that was evident in one of the speeches yesterday that you don't go up to somebody and say, "Hey, you're smoking. Well, I can help you fix that because you're presuming...it's insulting and it's intrusive.*

Great! She's heard this "suggestion" a couple of times already. Some say it takes 3 exposures to have an impact. (Jerry Kein liked "Direct Drive" suggestions and might repeat them 17 or more times.)

*K. (laugh) I had to learn, OK. I'm not telling you that I got here without a learning curve. I had to learn it.*

*J. I did that too.*

| | |
|---|---|
| *K. It helped me learn that we go in and out of trance states. So, as you've got that **confidence**...as **you're really sure of what you're doing**...you're **happy** and you're **open** and you're **ready to share**...how do you know you have that? How do you know that you're happy and open and ready to share?* | Looking for evidence SHE can use to believe in herself (using her words to keep her associated into the solution trance we want now.) |
| *J. Oh I just have a **lightness to my step**...you know, I **start the day eager to get going**, you know I don't really have any fear. **I'm pretty fearless**...and...and **I can conquer the world**.* | She's providing exactly what we need to suggest imaging that success |
| *K. Where and when do you want that?* | Looking for a specific reference. |
| *J. It'd be nice to have it all the time.* | |
| *K. And if you had it all the time would that be a good thing?* | Managing expectations. |
| *J. Oh, sure. Cause I feel like you could...you know...sort of **hit the switch on the up all night kind of sensation** if you needed to have down time. But, you know**, if you could turn it off and on at will that would be cool.*** | Thanks for the light switch metaphor! We'll use that later! |
| *K. What would you like to turn off and on at will?* | Again, looking for specifics for a clear understanding of a desired outcome. |

*J. Oh, that kind of manic state but that just kind of enthusiastic, happy...I'm just happy to be here and what can I help you with?*

*K. So, I'm curious, ok, because I heard you say that you want it all of the time but then you said you don't want it all of the time.*

*J. Well, I do want it all of the time but I'm sure that, you know,* ***you*** *have to recharge your batteries at some point, so...*

Making a personal preference/behavior global.

*K.* ***Own that****. You don't know if I have to recharge my batteries. Own that statement, rather than globalizing it so you have to say, "I have to recharge my batteries."*

Beginning to teach "only you can do it…no one can do it for you!"

*J. Well, I do. I have to recharge my batteries sometimes, but, I would like to have that down time be a little smaller than it is most of the time.*

And now she's "owning" her desire for down time too.

*K. So, I'm hearing you say that most of the time the switch is flipped off.*

*J. Or it's at least on dimmer mode and it's in the lower range, yeah.*

*K. So, then maybe what you would like to do is flip that other switch? The happy, upbeat...*

*J. Yeah, Yeah, I think that is energetically more attractive to others so I get into that vibe where clients would want what I had.*

*K. Tell me about that vibe...**how do you know you've got that vibe?** What is it?*

Continuing to look for specifics.

*J. Oh, it's just a happy energy, mostly. You just almost feel magnetic.*

*K. Oh, I saw you close your eyes...*

*J. Yeah, I know. I kinda had to access that feeling.*

*K. And when you did...when you closed your eyes and you <u>access that feeling</u>...where is it?*

She's about to tell us how to do it! (notice tense change to present)

*J. (sigh) Ah gosh, it's kinda...mostly in my heart area, I suppose. But I feel it all over. But that's where I feel the pull the most.*

Good kinesthetic reference

*K. This is confidence and exuberance and this is eagerness and this is all that...you're feeling all that right now?*

*J. Yeah!*

*K. How did you access that?*

What, specifically is the "process"?

| | |
|---|---|
| *J. I just felt like I was able to call it forth* | |
| *K. Where did you find it?* | Yes, and where is it? |
| *J. It was inside me all the time.* | Good discovery, 'Dorothy'! |
| *K. I watched you. You closed your eyes...* | |
| *J. And I pulled it out.* | Only SHE can do it! |
| *K. And, I'm curious, because we were talking about exuberance and that confidence and I asked you how would you know that...and this is what I saw you do...I'm not sure what you did but this is what I saw you do...you went (pantomime closing eyes and folding inward then opening eyes, sitting up straight with a big open smile...)* | |
| *J. Oh wow!* | |
| *K. So, I'm curious (pantomimes folding in)* | |
| *J. It was in the treasure chest that I keep locked up inside.* | Continuing her discovery of self! |
| *K. Ahhhh...how did you unlock that treasure chest just now?* | Might as well stick with her metaphor! |

*J. Well, it doesn't really have a "lock" lock on it. It opens pretty readily. But it stays closed for a lot of the time.*

*K. I asked you for it...and since I asked you for it, did that make it easier for you to open it up and get it?*

Referencing her external focus.

*J. Well absolutely cause I'm a sharing caring person by nature. So, if somebody wants something from me, I'm gonna give it to you.*

*K. I just heard you say any time someone comes up to you and wants or needs something from you, you can turn that switch right on*

Encouraging her to see her own abilities.

*J. That's probably accurate.*

*K. And, involved with others, you can flip that switch on as necessary.*

*J. True.*

*K. And it just absolutely happens.*

*J. Yep.*

*K. When you want it to happen.*

*J. Yep.*

*K. OK. So, what stops it from happening?*

Reality check!

*J. Well, isolation has been a really huge factor. I think the quarantine hit and that pretty-much shut me down.*

*And, I think I've kind of stayed a little closed off up until, well maybe about a month or so ago. You know, I thought, well this...we need to get the show on the road here and get moving and get things happening, so......*

*K. That down time that you had...that time that was kind of down...what did that do for you, Janet?*

What does the behavior do FOR you? (Every behavior has a positive intent!)

*J. It allowed me to kind of help gather more resources. I spent my quarantine down time doing some internet course work, catching up with some books I hadn't read. Got into some online courses and learning some things. More things to put in my toolbox.*

Exploring what she did for herself during that time.

*K. I'm curious. What resources do you already have for accumulating some confidence for creating this confidence in yourself...What resources do you already have?*

We're getting her beliefs! And resources we can call on to leverage change.

*J. I have* ***past life experience*** *and maybe past* ***LIVES*** *experiences, who knows, where I've done things or tried things and it turned out ok or I was successful at it. So,* ***I can tap into past successes***

Associating into the success trance.

*K. Do you have any you can tell me about?*

*J. Well, I was fascinated by some underwater photos that were shared with me at one time so I thought "I'm going to learn Scuba Diving." And I ended up getting probably every Scuba Certification that Patty offered...um...I'm a Master Scuba Diver cause I didn't go down the instructor track. I went down the skills track. And so, I've done* ***a lot of amazing Scuba dives.***

*K. And when you do those amazing Scuba Dives is it just because you're curious about that and you just want to do it. How do you get yourself ready for that? How do you know this is going to be an amazing experience?*

What is your evidence of "amazing"? (What, specifically is your process?)

*J.* ***Oh, I see it in my head****. I visualize what it is I'm going to see. I look through books or magazines. I got a couple of books on identifying fish that you might see in the ocean so that I'd be able to name them. I had an underwater camera, so I'd take pictures underwater. And then I'd look at those afterwards to reminisce about how wonderful it was...all the pretty things I saw, all the fish around the corals. I never knew fish were that intelligent and interactive. I always thought a fish is what you'd see in a*

Great! Pre-planning success rather than failure. That's a great "process" to encourage.

*fish tank in somebody's house or something. But they were like little puppy dogs. They'd come up to you and interact with you and check you out. Some would let you pet 'em. They'd absolutely let you feed them. It was a lot of fun.*

*K. (Laughing) It sounds like it was a lot of fun. All of that brought up confidence. If I heard you correctly, Janet...and correct me if I'm wrong cause I could mishear you...what I heard you say is that all the resources you have include* ***past lives*** *and what you can bring in from there.* ***You have success in your path****...that you have done a number of successful things in your past that you can look at and remember and think about. And you've got this one very specific visualization that you talked about and you also said that when you get eager about doing something that you* ***visualize*** *it, you* ***find out more*** *about it, you look for things about it and you get that picture in your head. That picture in your head of doing the Scuba Diving and all of that...tell me about that picture.*

Laughter is good! Healing! Remember to laugh with your clients!

Ego-strengthening suggestion.

Deepening the success trance. Repeating HER words.

Repeating her process back to her.

*J. I think probably* ***living the experience in my mind before I've even had it.*** *You know I get an expectation of 'here's what I'm gonna do' or 'here's what it's gonna feel like' or 'what it's going to smell like', this is*

That's also how she creates the self-doubt.

*what it's going to feel like...And I think I* ***often equate confidence with mastery****. So, if I'm able to do something well, it helps me feel confident.*

*K. I'm just curious. Is that a fair comparison? Mastery to confidence?*

Complex equivalence that needs challenging.

*J. No, No, but I think that competence and confidence are similar*

*K. Do you know anybody... can you think of anybody at the moment who has so much confidence it just fills the room but has little competence*

Unraveling a limiting belief.

*J. Oh yeah. Yeah. Any political figure.*

*K. So, I'm just curious if that is a fair assessment of the world.*

New reference point for her to gauge her belief.

*J. (Laughing) Ah, that's true! Good point!*

*K. I'm just curious if maybe that definition that you have given to confidence is skewed just a little bit.*

And as she rethinks it, she changes.

*J. Very much so. And it probably makes me hold myself to maybe a higher standard than maybe someone else might have as an expectation of how I might be.*

*K. Well don't ever, I don't ever want you to lower your expectations. Keep your high expectations, but I'd love for you to honor them. Let me just ask you this... when you park in a parking lot, do you park between the lines?*

*J. Oh absolutely, all the time.*

Great! Now we have an example to empower her to do her own ego-strengthening.

*K. And if you get out of your car and you're not between the lines, do you get back in and straighten it out?*

*J. Oh yeah.*

*K. Have you noticed that other people in the parking lot aren't quite as diligent as you are?*

*J. True. I usually park well away from them because I know they'll ding my doors.*

*K. But do you key their car or leave nasty note?*

*J. No, no. I just let it go.*

*K. You just let it go.*

Wouldn't it be nice to be as kind to yourself?

*J. They're just a bit more casual than me, I guess.*

*K. Yeah, **you're giving them sort of unconditional love**. But I wonder if you ever look back at your car and pat yourself on the back because you did such a great job?*

*J. No, not usually. But I might feel a little smug.*

*K. Listen to this, when you park between the lines you know what your non-verbal signals are to the world? What you're saying to the world every time you park right between those lines, what you're screaming to the world is: **I'm cooperative. I care about my stuff. I care about your stuff. I care about fairness.** We've all got enough room here, we can all get along. That's what you're screaming to the world.*

Showing how her actions are better than her self-talk.

*J. That's a good view, actually.*

*K. And do you ever stop to say, "I'm a good person. I really am a good parker. I really am a good citizen"?*

Suggestion for self-love.

*J. Yeah, I guess I could.*

*K. Would you?*

*J. Yeah, I would. I don't usually but I could.*

*K. Because you're, I believe, robbing yourself of some of the confidence that you deserve.*

Showing she has all the control in her own well-being - Positive or negative.

*J. Yeah, absolutely because I can be very self-critical.*

*K. Yeah. It's that little voice...there's no balance there. It's that little voice that spends all its time criticizing and none of its time*

*J. Praising and rewarding.*

There's the awareness and understanding of what can be changed.

*K. Taking stock of what you do well. So, there's a little bit of confusion there about whether you're any good or not. And that little inner child there who wants good things for you. All that little one wants is to be praised.*

Even without "formal trance," she's still positively hallucinating the little one.

*J. Absolutely.*

*K. And hugged. After all, when she was little she had a big brother and sister and mom who told her mean things sometimes.*

*J. Yeah, I was actually the oldest, everybody was younger so I kind of had to always be the responsible person and if anything ever went wrong it was always my fault.*

Be careful of your assumptions...but even that mistake doesn't break this trance...

*K. And if anything went right...whose fault was that?*

*J. Uh, Mom's.*

Referring back to the voices.

*K. (Laugh) So, there are those voices always saying you're doing it wrong...are they right?*

*J. Ummmmm no, but sometimes, you know, it was only because even negative attention is better than no attention.*

*K. I got that. I understand that absolutely, so that's where you downloaded that program, right? You downloaded that program 'it's better to get negative attention than no attention at all'. So, you downloaded that program and that little one inside of you who wants that positive attention...*

*J. Hey, it takes what it can get.*

*K. Is willing to criticize self because it's the only attention it's gettin'. I wonder what might happen if that little one inside got some of that praise.*

Not "suggesting" the change...just wondering to let her decide.

| | |
|---|---|
| *J. Whew...I'm not sure she'd know what to do. (Laugh)* | |
| *K. I'll bet she would because we already know her M.O. Her M.O.is open and sharing and giving. So, we know exactly what she'll do.* | Associating her into the effects of positive self-talk. |
| *J. Oh yeah, she'd skip and dance and laugh and have fun.* | |
| *K. I'm curious why she's not getting that.* | Let the client decide. |
| *J. I need to talk to myself more, I guess.* | Yes, in positive ways! |
| *K. Yeah, but let's start small, can we? Can we start small.* | Encouraging her to change the things she can...now! |
| *J. Sure.* | |
| *K. And, from now on, when you park between the lines in a parking lot, will you take a moment just to say, "That says wonderful things about you. You are really good at being cooperative. Thank you for being so cooperative".* | Wide awake post hypnotic suggestion. To be repeated in the "Formal Hypnosis" session. |
| *J. Yeah, that's a gold star moment.* | |
| *K. Do you return phone calls?* | More suggestions for positive self-talk. |
| *J. Oh absolutely, I always do, yes.* | |

*K. Always?*

*J. Unless it's a spammer or a sales call. I get a lot of those right now.*

*K. And here we go again. Do you pat yourself on the back for being good at returning phone calls?*

*J. It's something I take pride in, yes.*

*K. Good, and do you actually praise yourself for that?*

*J. No, I guess I don't. But I could, I should, I will!*

More agreement to change.

*K. So, those are little things. Do you show up on time for appointments?*

*J. I'm early for things. That's a motto of mine, early is on time, on time is late and late is unacceptable*

*K. So, when you show up early, do you show up and tap your foot and say, "I'm here. Let's get started." Or do you bring a book or your phone or keep yourself occupied until the time.*

Association to the things she does well that may be unappreciated.

*J. I keep myself occupied. Or chat with anyone who's willing to chat.*

*K. And for **being responsible for yourself**. For giving yourself something to do...in not imposing yourself on anyone...Has she ever*

Repeating the reality check that she is the one who deserves credit...

*been thanked for that?*

*J. No*

*K. Has she ever been praised for that?*

*J. Uh, no.*

*K. I wonder what might happen if she were...*

*J. Aw, it would be pretty happy stuff.*

*K. I wonder if we could grow her confidence by giving her a little bit of praise.*

Utilizing her natural desire to help "others", let's see if she can do it for the "little one".

*J. That'd be awesome. Those are great baby steps.*

*K. And as you grow her confidence, you know what that does*

*J. It makes the rest of me confident, and it explodes...*

She's a quick study!

*K. All over the place because right now you told me she would rather have negative attention than no attention at all.*

*J. True.*

*K. And since she's not getting any praise...*

| | |
|---|---|
| *J. Well, positive praise would be best. Certainly, negative praise wouldn't be better than no praise.* | She is well-connected now to that inner child |
| *K. She's settling for the negative voices that keep coming up because it's attention.* | |
| *J. Well, yeah, that's all there is. I just need to put a muffle on that and start listening more to the good angel on the other shoulder.* | As she decides how to handle this change. |
| *K. Guess what, this will be muffled as you increase the praise over here.* | |
| *J. Yeah.* | |
| *K. The two voices cannot live at the same time. They can't be heard at the same time* | Suggestion for more positive self-talk. |
| *J. True.* | |
| *K. And the little one already told us that she would settle for negative attention just to get some attention.* | |
| *J. Yep.* | |
| *K. And the only one now...the only one now... who can give her that positive attention...who can parent her the way she deserves to be parented is you. And the only one who can do it is you.* | Suggestions for taking responsibility. |
| *To put up sticky notes on the refrigerator, "Praise Yourself". "Compliment yourself". Or you could* | *Suggestion using her visualization* |

technique.

*actually keep some sort of gratitude journal. Every morning you could wake up and visualize the things you're going to accomplish. And you could, at night before going to sleep, praise yourself for the things you did right today. And I don't mean winning the lottery, I mean praise yourself for...I noticed that that woman was coming out of the grocery store with her arms full and I held the door open for her. I did that because I'm an observant person and I care about people. And maybe...maybe the only thing that goes right today is that you're walking along the street and you happen to notice a penny...and you reach down and you pick it up...and it's heads up...and its shiny...and you can say, "This appeared from the universe just for me". If I find a penny on the ground, I celebrate right there, "Woohoohoo! Look what the universe put in my path right now". And it's sounds ridiculous, but...*

Suggestion for ongoing self-praise.

Offering options for noticing what's going right.

*J. Naw, I pick up every penny even if tails up. That's an angel talking to you.*

And we'll call on those angels if we need to!

*K. There you go. And do you celebrate that angel talking to you?*

*J. I do.*

*K. And that little one...look what they brought just to us today. That little one*

Conversational Inner Child Work.

| | |
|---|---|
| *inside of you...that little one inside of you. I wonder Janet, I wonder if you can imagine her and how old she is.* | Wide-awake yet she can positively hallucinate the child. |
| *J. She's 3.* | See. |
| *K. Can we take that little 3-year old and put her over here on the floor? Just put her over here on the floor for a minute.* | |
| *J. OK.* | |
| *K. Look at her...look at her on the floor. Look at her down there...is there anything wrong with her?* | |
| *J. Oh, no. She's cute!* | Confirmation of positive hallucination. |
| *K. She's adorable, isn't she?* | |
| *J. Yeah, she's got my little...well, I wasn't 3 when I got it...but she's got my little pink ballet costume on.* | Reality came in, but she let that go and continued with her hallucination. |
| *K. And she's just age-appropriate and doing everything she can to just be happy...be energized...be open...be sharing, is she not?* | Deepening the trance with her positive words. |
| *J. Yep.* | |
| *K. Tell her how cute she is.* | |

| | |
|---|---|
| *J. Oh, you're so cute.* | As she looks and talks to the little one, the trance deepens. |
| *K. Tell her what you're impressed about her for...what about her impresses you* | |
| *J. She's got a great smile.* | |
| *K. Don't tell me...tell her.* | |
| *J. You've got such a cute smile...and your curly hair is so cute.* | And she looks right at the spot where she placed the little one. |
| *K. What does she do when you tell her that?* | |
| *J. She kinda closes her eyes and giggles. (Laughs)* | Dissociated view of younger self. |
| *K. (Laughing) It might be attention she's not used to.* | Staying in the tranced with her. Hallucinating that little one based on client feedback. |
| *J. That's right.* | |
| *K. But she giggled...so she likes it. She might have closed her eyes because she's not used to it...but she giggled...she likes it. I wonder what she can do when she gets that more often. I wonder how she's going to* | Staying in the trance with her. Hallucinating that little one based on client feedback. |

*grow into appreciating positive attention.*

*J. I'm sure she'll find it a lot easier than I do.*

*K. Well ask her.*

*J. How would that feel? Oh, you'd love it! OK.*

Getting feedback from the little one.

*K. If you wanna give her a hug and incorporate her back into you...you can do that. Let her know that you love her...and that you're here to take care of her...and if no one else praises her...you will do it.*

Respecting the trance. A part of her is now outside of herself, metaphorically speaking.

*J. (Holding herself and swaying back and forth) I got you girl.*

Noticeable connection.

*K. Don't tell her that if it's not true cause she'll know if you're lying to her.*

*J. I'm not lyin'. I got you. We'll be a power force...that's what we'll be.*

Noticeable connection.

*K. Isn't that a wonderful thing.*

*J. Oh my gosh.*

*K. Isn't that a wonderful thing. Now, you have so many resources, Janet. You have that little one. You have that cute little one in the pink suit with your curls and her cute smile. You have her to be grateful for because, you know what, she put up with all the crap all*

Repeating the discoveries.

Taking her current habits all the way

*along the way. And she just kept going like the energizer bunny.*

back to her younger self.

*J. That's true.*

*K. And every day she knew to just keep going. And because of what she went through and everybody else after her went through they got you here today. If they hadn't put up with all of the stuff, you wouldn't be here today. But they did...so they deserve some gratitude...all of 'em. Some praise and gratitude. Because they persevered...they came through. You've got <u>past life experience</u>...you've got <u>books and magazines</u> to look through...you've got a <u>vivid imagination</u> so you can <u>imagine how you want something to go even in the future</u>. You have all of those resources already in your toolkit...do you need any other resources?*

Moving the learnings forward.

Meanwhile the client can allow her story to change.

Bringing her strengths along for the ride.

*J. I have a ton of resources. Someone once told me I would be selfish if I didn't share them. (tears)*

Tears are a great sign of recognition. (Re-Cognition)

*K. So, you don't need any additional resources, you've got a lot and you're not selfish. If there's any incongruity going on it's because you're open and eager.*

*J. That's right.*

| | |
|---|---|
| *K. So why are you holding all these resources to yourself?* | Don't assume...ask. |
| *J. (Big sigh) I was afraid.* | Understanding. |
| *K. Well, I don't know. Were you afraid, Janet or was she afraid?* | |
| *J. She was afraid.* | More reason to love her/self. |
| *K. Because no one's been praising her.* | Linking the problem to the solution. |
| *J. That's right.* | |
| *K. And the only one she cares about is you. The only one she wants to love her...is you.* | Linking the solution to the one who can affect the change. |
| *J. Aw. (hugging herself and patting her shoulders)* | Sign of acceptance. |
| *K. And she will grow in confidence and grow in maturity and grow in everything else when she gets that positive attention...that love from you. You have the capacity to love her, do you not?* | Desired outcome. |
| *J. I do. Here we got her, Hello Kitty. (Holding up a stuffed Hello Kitty plush toy)* | |
| *K. There ya go. That (nodding) yes. And the way you looked at Hello Kitty...look at Hello Kitty and imagine you're looking at that little 3-year old* | She offered up the physical element, so why not use it! |

*girl. And let her see that love coming out of your eyes...cause I can see it.*

*J. (Laughing)*

*K. And let it reflect back into you. So, Janet, I'm curious...to* ***flip that switch of confidence on****...imagine it like a light switch. You know, when we flip a light switch off...which in isolation some of us did...we turned it off and said "wait till this passes"...and when we turn a light on...we don't ever have to worry about it. You don't have to worry about that light going off right? You flipped it on...and until you come back to that light switch and flip it off, it's gonna stay on, isn't it?*

Repeating the metaphor she offered and turning it in to a technique she can use to create what she wants.

*J. Yes.*

*K. Well, what happens if you flip that on...flip that on...but not all the time, because there are some times when you want to relax. There are some times when you just want to be quiet. Sometimes when you don't wanna be sitting in your pajamas at home and calling a neighbor saying, "I just have something I have to share with you." You just want to be in your pajamas at home, right? So, sometimes you can flip it off.*

A little guided visualization of using the technique.

*J. Yeah.*

*K. But those times that you want it...as*

Rehearsing the

*you visualize it...flip that on...praise that little one and imagine what might happen.*

technique.

*J. Magic.*

Results!

*K. What is the first step to getting there, Janet? What's your first step to take to get there...the baby steps?*

She'll provide the suggestions she's willing to accept.

*J. Uh...I will remember to* ***praise the little steps****. To* ***be happy for the little wins****.* ***When things go right it's like "Woo Hoo, boy that was great!"*** *And to* ***thank her and to send her love every day.***

Thanks for writing the script!

*K. Is there more than one way to get there?*

Choice is better than no choice.

*J. Oh no, there's all kinds of ways.*

*K. And is there another way that you can think of that would be efficient?*

Give them time to figure it out.

*J. (Long Pause) To just to know...*

*K. To know...finish that sentence.*

I need some clarity.

*J. Just* ***to know that I am enough****.* ***That I'm strong and I can do whatever I set my mind to.***

Reinforce the things she can believe!

*K. And do you suppose you're just gonna wake up every morning with that knowledge over the next week or so or...*

Getting specific...

*J. No, **I need to write it down**. I keep a gratitude journal but I've been lax lately about doing it twice a day, I only do it once a day now. And I got out of the habit of **doing my evening wins**. I had learned that you should start to kinda like **'what are my wins today' and then celebrate those**. So, I'll return to that.*

More for the script!

*K. And can we add to it gratitude and praise journal. Personal Praise Journal.*

*J. **Personal Praise**, absolutely.*

*K. You don't have to show it to everybody...although you can...*

*J. But if you're not getting strokes anywhere else, I guess you gotta stroke yourself.*

Re-Cognition.

*K. Plus, if you write it down, she might believe it.*

*J. It's true.*

*K. Do it diligently and imagine how exponentially she can grow.*

Direct suggestion for continued action.

*J. Uh huh...*

*K. She's in this with you.*

*J. Uh huh!*

*K. There's no resistance.*

*J. Well she's got a vested interest because she's carried around inside me all the time.*

Good belief to utilize.

*K. She's right there...as a matter of fact, if you want to...if you need her exuberance or her innocence...or her desire to please or her desire to do something...all you have to do is tap right here...*

Suggesting a kinesthetic anchor and utilizing her skill of doing things for others.

*J. Yeah.*

*K. Or wherever you incorporated her, she's right there.*

*J. Yep.*

*K. She'll go with you. She'll be there to remind you. "Hey, what about me?" And when you notice those negative voices going off in your head...do you notice that when it happens?*

Suggesting she is "working for someone else" because she is willing to share and has an external locus of control.

*J. Usually.*

*K. You can talk to her here or you can take her out and put her on the floor and say, "I'm sorry. I've been really mean to you. Let's rethink this." And get back in touch with her value..her worth...her strength for just being.*

*J. Yeah.*

*K. How cool is that?*

*J. That's really cool.*

That workshop demo is also a good example of how a typical intake might go in my office. I get to watch the change happen and conversationally check to make sure the client is moving in the direction they desire. I also gather a wealth of information to use in the formal hypnosis and subsequent sessions as necessary.

The questions work really well to move a mindset from problem to solution. And lend themselves well to doing on-the-fly interventions such as regression to resources or simple parts negotiation. When working with issues of trauma such as abuse or PTSD, I'm not a big fan of Regression to Cause that leads to revivification or re-living the trauma to facilitate the healing. There are no examples in the transcripts here of a dissociated review, but, with trauma, I prefer an observational perceptional position. That's where the client imagines rising above their timeline and as an observer notices what's happening at significant spots along the timeline below them.

We're working with imagination, so once it's suggested, it's easily accomplished:

> *Rise above the chair you're sitting in until you can look down and see yourself sitting there. Let me know when you're there.*
>
> *Good! Notice the line of time running through you from the beginning of time for you all the way into the future. As you observe that timeline, you'll notice a sign or a flag marking significant issues. Float over the first one you come to and tell me what's happening down there.*

When you're in rapport with your client, it's just that easy. But, if you prefer deep trance for the timeline work, induce hypnosis and then proceed with the suggestion to rise above the chair. You may choose to use ideomotor signals or interactive conversation to gather your client's responses. As my friend Jess Marion says, "Either way is better."

While the observer position lends itself to gathering important info without having to relive the trauma, sometimes you want to work with the emotions as they present. And if that is confusing, please get adequate regression/timeline training. One quick tip, since we're working with the imagination, when necessary, I calmly tell my client:

> *There's a drain underneath that scene you're observing. That's the "emotional drain." So, you can allow all of that emotion to drain out of that scene now. Take a good long breath...and let it all drain out with your exhale. Let go of the emotion, but let's keep the learning. Now, as you observe that scene...what is to be discovered here?*

As you already know, it's a dance. I lead with a question. The client responds with their best answer. I take the next step based on that response.

Before you leave the dance of curiosity and information gathering, you might want to enhance your language with the client's personal trance words; these are values held close to their core. In the demo with Janet, I noted pride, happy, open, somebody likes me, share, teach, lightness of step, eager. Remember each client is unique and these words resonate deeply and represent the clients benefits/leverage for change.

Sometimes you'll discover plenty to work with in an outcome conversation. But if you want to go even farther, you'll like the upcoming section on Personal Trance words that can beef up any session or script. Remember, your goal is to empower the client to do all the work. After all, you're working in their head and they're going to take that with them when they leave! And hopefully they'll remain empowered to support the change when they leave your session and keep dancing.

CHAPTER 10:

# THE PERFORMANCE

I've mentioned "formal hypnosis" several times. Sometimes hypnotists do their intake and then "get permission" to hypnotize the client before moving into the "therapy" part of the session. That's wasted time in my opinion. Therapy, in this case, DOES NOT imply psychoanalysis because most of our clients aren't "psycho"! We're working, as the National Guild of Hypnotists says, "with ordinary people who have ordinary problems." (Anything beyond your scope of practice should be referred to someone who is qualified to help.)

As you can see from the "Janet transcript," I was simply working with curiosity and a set of questions designed to get specific about a stated goal and the steps it takes to get there. My goal in each session is to facilitate the client in designing THEIR route to their desired outcome.

So, I don't wait until we move to the "magic change chair" to start the session. I'm dancing with my client with every contact.

- The dance starts when the client gets in the mood/mindset to change (dance) and looks for a partner.

- The invitation to <u>dance with me</u> is on my website, on social media, in all speeches or other encounters.

- I get a <u>nod</u> (or slight smile) when the prospective client calls inquiring about sessions, mentoring or training.

- I get <u>compliance</u> when we schedule the appointment.

- Permission comes when the invoice is paid prior to the appointment.

Rapport has already been established and will continue as the dance moves right into the question: What do you want to change today? And the "therapy" works in tandem with the discovery. It often works even better than "formal hypnosis" because the client has no idea hypnosis is happening (although it most definitely is!) so there's no need for resistance. The suggestions, reframing, metaphor, etc., are encoded quite organically.

If we've been great partners, my client continues to use the dance steps and may return for more sessions to create new routines. If the client decides to ignore THEIR OWN suggestions and continues to do the old, limited dance, that also is their choice. Remember, we each have the right to map our own reality. I take responsibility for being the best facilitator I can possibly be. The responsibility for actually doing the change is with the client.

If I get an indication along the way that regression will produce resources, I'll do an eyes-open regression right there while we're talking about it. The client is obviously already associated into it, so why wait? I'm looking for resources the client has used in the past to create success. And I'll get all the suggestions necessary for client integration.

Now, of course, I observe for any signs of abreaction, because anything can trigger positive or negative thoughts or memories. But it's a very rare client who will associate into negatives when we're actively regressing for resources. If a client does come up with a negative in that wide-awake regression, the dance simply continues. I take the feedback and deal with it there. It's quite apparent in that case that we've danced our way into something the client needs to handle. And we work with it appropriately. It is always a dance of give and take. Observe and react. And remember that crying is NOT abreacting. Crying is getting in touch with feelings. An abreaction is actually a total split with the personality. As long as you're working within your scope of practice, there's little chance of that happening.

Parts work is indicated in the same way. And often I talk to the parts as soon as they're mentioned. However, understand, it's a dance designed to make the client look and feel as good as possible. Sometimes along the way in the discovery process, I make notes of work that is better left until the "formal" hypnosis or until a subsequent session.

After the conversational change work/intake, I wrap it all up with a typical eyes-closed hypnosis session based entirely off of what was learned from the client. Since I've already used a variety of NLP techniques, metaphor, conversational regression, inner-child work, or whatever it takes to affect the change before the client "knows" they're being hypnotized by their own revelations, the "formal hypnosis" is easy. It includes patter, direct suggestion, metaphor, story, etc., predicated on the client's discovered solutions.

From what we learned with Janet, let's explore how to turn that into "formal hypnosis."

You'll have to calibrate with your client to discover the "trance induction" you'll use. Since I believe that we're always in trance, for me, all it takes is the intention to go into hypnosis and I'm there. But I have some clients who have specific beliefs about what a "deep trance" experience is for them, and so, for them, I'll spend some time on muscle relaxation and a countdown deepener to stay in rapport with their expectations. Either way is better! Janet proved she easily goes into trance, even with her eyes open. So, I'll keep it easy and highlight a possible "script" that unfolds from our chat.

*Janet, just take a nice breath and as you exhale, settle yourself into that wonderful state of hypnosis...where your mind can wander and explore.......*

*and begin now to visualize your success.*

*I don't know if you're scuba diving...or teaching...or seeing clients...I don't know...but you know where and when you have that confidence.*

*If you happen to notice any self-doubt along the way...erase it.*

*Hmmmm, I don't know what you're imagining...but I find it kind of interesting that I see a big pink eraser...like we had in elementary school...a big one that lets you erase self-doubt...Just erase it...wipe it away. It's interesting what the mind can do, is it not?*

*Negative comments from any voice...even your own...negative thoughts...negative concepts...negative self-talk about being good enough...Ha! Anyone with a voice like that just doesn't really know you, do they?*

*So, pause for a moment...turn down that negative sound and consider the source. What went wrong for them that they have doubt? ...Maybe they don't know the truth...maybe they haven't yet appreciated your skills and abilities. Maybe they haven't appreciated yet...how you are eager to learn and share...maybe they haven't yet appreciated how you compare quite favorably to your peers...because you know the truth...somebody likes you! And when you visualize yourself eager...fearless...ready to give and share...happy...and open to conquering the world...you ARE fearless! And you are good!*

*Now, if I were to ask you to help me find the solution to self-doubt, I know you would confidently flip the switch and give me your very best.*

*Pause for a moment and visualize flipping on that switch of confidence...eager to share and give...you know you can do it...all you have to do is journey back through time...past lives...past experiences...past successes. Take a moment to really see, hear and feel how it feels to flip on the confidence and feel the success...The pride...the confidence...you did it!*

*You can do it!*

*Collect as many examples of your success as you can...and hold them out in front of you to examine one by one...to feel...one-by-one...to hear the compliments...one-by-one...each one building to the you of today. Each one giving you a learning experience...and personal experience...and wisdom...and something wonderful to share.*

*Notice how good it feels to know you have something to share.*

*Imagine that little one...3...in her pink outfit...that smile...those curls...and look at her with the unconditional love that she deserves.*

*Appreciate her for going through whatever she had to go through...and yet, she persisted! She hung in there. And all the other earlier versions of you...persisted...each bringing something valuable to the you of today.*

*Take a moment to visualize that collective success...feel it...hear it!*

*Pull it into you...and notice the lightness in your step...I wonder how you're standing as you realize you can conquer the world...how are you breathing...what's the look on your face?*

*Visualize yourself taking that confidence into your future...when you can use it the most.*

*And won't that be wonderful to write down! Visual proof of your accomplishments building your confidence more and more as the days turn into weeks and the weeks turn into months.*

*Tell yourself now that you will do a review of each day and write down your wins... celebrating every single win little and big...and reminding that little one how precious she is...as she looks up to you to remind you how grateful she is to you...and proud of you for getting her all the way to now...as you notice the lightness of step while you both go confidently into your bright and happy future.*

*Stay with that as long as you'd like...and when you're ready to confidently open your eyes and expand your horizons...flip the switch and return to the here and now.*

That's one example of turning her words into a script and utilizing the "therapy" we've already done to create a powerful installation or "formal" session.

Realize, if you prefer a more classic style of hypnosis, you can do The Elman Induction, or progressive muscle relaxation or guided visualization plus deepening and then use the client's words and strategies as the direct suggestion, add the post hypnotic suggestion(s) and emerge your client.

You can do Age Regression (Affect Bridge, Time/Place, Symptom, Cognitive) with the information you discover from the client while they're still wide awake. You can do parts work on the spot or perhaps use the information to map a strategy for subsequent sessions dealing with the various aspects of an issue. You can use

NLP techniques, EFT, angel readings, past life regression, crystals, essential oils, etc., whatever technique you're trained to use to affect the change and your client believes will help them make the change.

One thing you can count on by framing your client in the best possible light and giving them space to specifying their outcome and strategies is: you are working in their head rather than trying to persuade clients to work with your perceptions or rules.

(If you'd like to take a deep dive into the concepts, nuances and client calibration used in wide-awake hypnosis, add The Hypnotic Coach: A Conversational Hypnotherapy Tool Kit by Jess Marion to your library.)

And while we took a look here at the "technical" part of the dance, there's more to add some pizzazz and even some leverage for change.

Shall we continue?

CHAPTER 11:

# PERSONAL TRANCE TANGO

The Outcome Specification demo proved to give us plenty of information about Janet to create a great session. But sometimes, a few more easy questions are needed to elicit value words from the client. And when you use their words, there is no need for resistance. In fact, the client will give you the words that mean the most to them.

These extra questions can be used to break a state, as I did with the boyfriend question in the Janet demonstration. Her answer about the boyfriend included "somebody likes me" which could branch off into a session about how she could tell he likes her and how she can go looking for that each time she shares her information with someone (as an example). Or it could lead to a session on gaining a more internal locus of control. Or maybe you notice something different. In any case, that simple answer reveals something about Janet's core values.

An easy set of questions to have handy include:

- What do you need in a job for it to be enjoyable?

- How do you know you've done a good job at something?
- What makes a friendship/relationship meaningful?
- What's your hobby? What draws you to that hobby?
- What's the most relaxing place you can think of?

Here's a transcript from another demo in the Mid-America Virtual Conference workshop that focuses specifically now on eliciting Personal Trance Words. Notice how much we can learn with some easy questions. If you'd like to watch while reading, go to KarenHand.com/Trance-Dance.

| | |
|---|---|
| *K. What do you need in a job for it to be enjoyable?* | |
| *D.* ***Personal Satisfaction****.* | Internal locus of control. |
| *K. How do you know you've done a good job at something?* | |
| *D. I* ***feel it deep inside*** *me.* | Kinesthetic |
| *K. How do you know?* | |
| ***D. Warm. Happy. Accomplished. Pride.*** | That's a nice list of personal trance words! |
| *K. Aw, good. Excellent. In a relationship, a friendship, something like that, what has to be in that friendship for it to be of value to you?* | |
| *D.* ***Truth and loyalty****.* | We'll use these again to reinforce |

the suggestions.

*K. Aw...good. What's your hobby?*

*D. Writing...stories.*

We'll use these again to reinforce the suggestions.

*K. What draws you to that?*

*D. I've just always had a very* ***creative mind****. I've* ***journaled*** *since I was a child. I have dream journals from when I was like 11. I've just always...the first ever book I wrote came off a past-life regression I did about 14 years ago.*

Great tip for a technique to use where she re-writes her story/history/future.

*K. How cool is that! What's the most relaxing place you can think of?*

*Tip! Journaling will be good homework for her with focused attention on the goal.

*D. In Glastonbury, England Chalice Well* ***Gardens****.*

*K. Lovely!*

When you are curious (asking questions) they will give you what you need as far as words, technique, metaphor, etc.)

Now, I didn't get a "personal trance word" from Dee by asking about her favorite place of relaxation, but, what I did get is a great metaphor. If I were to do a guided visualization as an induction to formal trance or for a "Mental Massage with Karen" session, I wouldn't do a beach scene. But telling her a story about walking through a garden would be a fairly direct route to her relaxation.

Some people will give rather detailed descriptions of their relaxing/favorite place including sounds, smells, tastes, temperature, etc. Others are as succinct as Dee saying things such as “in my bed surrounded by pillows,” “in the mountains,” etc. It's usually better to ask than to guess.

Dee might have a great session leading off with a story about floating on a raft in calm Caribbean waters, then again, she might be afraid of water. So, why not just stick with what she told us, build rapport, and get the job done.

What I get from asking the personal trance questions – either sporadically through the intake conversation or simply in order – is another set of the client's words that speak to what is valued. You don't even need to know subject matter or specifics when you have the client's personal trance words. Keep your suggestions vague and let the client do the work.

Full disclosure, my preferred representational system is auditory, so it's most efficient for me to hear it in the client's words. That's why I prefer to have a conversation or go down a list of questions. You may prefer a visual representation. If so, add these questions to your intake form and you can read all about it for clues to build rapport and help your client reach a goal. You can even do that ahead of time if you have the time to spend preparing for your client. I operate best on the fly, so conversational change feels natural to me. You will arrange the information-gathering technique that works best for you in your office.

In Dee's case, realize we don't have an “issue” (or my preferred “specifics”), but we can use some common sense and give her a quickie trance. Remember, this is happening in a class she chose to take at a conference. Utilizing the learning trance she's already in, it might be something like this:

> *As we sit here together in this electronic learning environment, just take a nice breath and on the exhale...close your eyes.... That's right.*

*And you can begin to reflect on all the information you're taking in...some brand new tidbits...some confirmation of what you already know...and it's amazing...you can feel so good deep inside as you recognize more and more the personal satisfaction you get by moving toward your loftiest goals.*

*Imagine yourself now as if you're there...you have accomplished what you want...that warm...happy feeling of knowing you always give it your best. You're open to learning new things and you take pride in your abilities to do...not just what you ought to do each day...but notice the personal satisfaction it brings to you deep, deep inside as you discover the truth.*

*At the very moment of conception, you won the race for life...and as you journey from that moment forward, feel the pride welling up deep inside as you realize you have done the very best you can each and every step along the way. Using your creative mind to cultivate the garden you call your life. Notice how you've nurtured every seed that brings you personal satisfaction...tending each blossom that makes you happy along the way...keeping that which works for you...just like that feeling of pride as you took your first step...rode your bike without training wheels...graduation...personal satisfaction.*

*And as you stay true and loyal to your most-precious desires...you know the truth...and the truth is...you can write the story of your success.*

*Take a moment to feel the success...take in the pride...and decide now to accomplish that which brings you the very most personal satisfaction...because it feels so good!*

*Take as long as you like with that wonderful warm and happy feeling...and when you're ready to accomplish even more...return to the here and now feeling ready to take the next step.*

An entire script simply utilizing the "learning trance" inherent in a convention workshop and the personal trance words discovered with a few simple questions. That "script" is so vague that the client has space to reflect on what she's learned in this class or this conference or she may choose to focus on some other goal that brings satisfaction. Either way she's encouraged to focus on her ability to succeed at whatever she desires.

Imagine what can be done with all of the specific information you gather from your client.

I have a couple of handy forms I use with clients which work just fine for one-session wonders, and also prove quite helpful when the client returns for a subsequent session, or even a year later to work on something different. You can download printable handouts for techniques mentioned in this book at KarenHand.com/Trance-Dance.

CHAPTER 12:

# THE GRAND FINALE

Remember, the dance with your client started long before your first words or eye contact.

Going back to that Dancing with the Stars analogy, the celebrities know who their pro will be before they arrive for the first meeting. The celeb has time to get excited and imagine how well they will do under the professional tutelage of their assigned partner. That's building expectation. The same thing happens for your client between the time they schedule the appointment and have their session. They have hope for a solution.

In the case of a hypnosis client, you can presume they've done their research. Even if they just closed their eyes and pointed to a name on a google list, you don't get to judge. Whatever they did to choose you as their hypnotist is the appropriate level of research for that particular person. Of course, your job is even easier if you're chosen because the client saw you in action, or because they reacted favorably to a video, or because you've been recommended by a doctor or trusted friend. Those elements can go a long way in building prestige and enhancing the session experience. No matter how you were selected, notice that YOU WERE HIRED! And you can trust that the client is doing the very best they can with the information they have about you and hypnosis. So, when they show up in person or online, they're expecting to get some relief.

As you maintain the curiosity frame, you build rapport with the client. And just like the pro on the dancing show, it's up to you to find out what skills your Trance Dance Partner already has to build upon and then discover what the client can do to create their successful outcome.

Now, Dancing with the Stars has one additional element. Judges are there to rate the routine. Sometimes the judges are unyielding and downgrade a performance because it broke the strict rules of that particular dance style.

Breathe a sigh of relief now! You don't have to worry about such rigid rules. In fact, you'll do well to practice these questions and put them into your style. When you have this conversation with your client, you'll stay on track to find just what you need to facilitate the requested change. Instead of being overly concerned about getting in all of the questions, or getting them in perfect order, keep your eyes and ears on the client. Throw out the rules and look and listen for what can change now and what needs further exploration to create the desired result.

The best way to listen is to STOP TALKING! So, ask your questions, and then be present for the answer. When you look and listen, you will instinctively apply the best approach you know to promote the desired result.

For a binary change, a simple yes or no, I like to use a standard fork-in-the-road technique. During the intake, I discover a client's reasons for making the change, the benefits they'll reap by making the change, and the steps they're prepared to take to get there. All of that information is available with the Outcome Questions. A copy of this simple fork-in-the-road metaphor in script form is available at KarenHand.com/Trance-Dance.

You'll know age regression might be the right technique when your client says, "I know when the issue started" or they regress physically or vocally as they tell the story or when their reaction is far bigger than the stimulus. When this occurs during the questioning, you can simply say, "Tell me more about that" and it will instantly deepen their trance.

Decide first if you want to complete the regression work then and there or if you want to wait until the "formal trance" to discover more about the issue. Some hypnotists choose deep trance regression-to-cause to look for the "Initial Sensitizing Event." Some do the change work with a "Subsequent Sensitizing Events" or even a "Recent Sensitizing Event." There are so many ways to affect a change. You will choose the facilitation method that you believe will work. The beauty of Outcome Specification and direction toward a goal is that this information is valuable no matter what modality you're using. It adds the necessary client information for hypnosis, NLP, EFT, energy work, acupuncture, card readings, etc., where the intended outcome is client-centered and positive. And it naturally points the client toward a solution mindset.

There is no right or wrong decision on whether you do your fancy techniques along the way or wait until the trance event later. That's a choice based on personal preference and training. Except, if you do the dance of regression at any point, be sure you're well-trained in what to do once you get to an event whether it's an ISE, SSE, or RSE. You're suggesting the client manipulate perceptions and beliefs to change on a deep level. So, make sure you're properly trained in regression, re-imprinting, inner child work, anger issues and even forgiveness before leading someone down that road. Regression isn't necessary for every issue by any means. But it can be a healing adventure for many clients when done well.

A Regression Handout is provided at KarenHand.com/Trance-Dance with tips on when to use regression, conversational inductions and questions that avoid leading the client into false memories. Also, if you need additional training in Age Regression,

Re-imprinting, or inner-child work, you can reach me at Karen@KarenHand.com.

Parts Work shows up the same way in that intake conversation. Janet said she had negative self-talk and realized the voice wasn't hers; in fact, she said it may be several people. That's an indication that we might want to talk with those parts and find out their positive intent. It might be a place to mediate a change in self-perception if the "formal" direct suggestion process isn't sufficient. For a Parts Work Handout, you know where to go: KarenHand.com/Trance-Dance.

Understand, I am in no way implying that Janet, our demo subject, needs regression, parts work, or any other technique. I'm just pointing out what was noted about this "session." It was a demonstration. In the "real world," I would ask a client for feedback on their success. And, by the way, I have Janet's feedback that I'll share in a moment.

When a client has unresolved anger issues, I most often use forgiveness techniques to erode and dissolve the need for anger. The Gestalt Empty Chair technique proves to be so useful here as well as other issues where the client needs to air their grievances. Here's an example of how I might explain it:

> *Forgiveness isn't at all for the person who wronged you. It's not about forgiving and forgetting. I mean, after all, if you forget, you might be vulnerable to it again. This forgiveness is about getting that anger out of your body. Anger is like taking poison yet hoping the other person will suffer. This is about getting that poison out of you.*
>
> *So, put an empty chair across the room from you. And install a forcefield of safety and protection between you and that other chair. You can make that forcefield out of anything you like. Anything on the other side of that forcefield is obligated to listen to you and hear all of your thoughts and feelings...but they can't do anything to you. They're on the*

*other side of that forcefield. The only thing that will ever come back to your side of the forcefield is what you personally allow on your side.*

*So, now imagine (<u>that person who hurt you</u>) in that chair. And tell them everything they ever did to you to hurt you...and how it made you feel...and how it still hurts you today. Confront them with everything... Let it go.*

The client may choose to have their rant out loud or silently. If they're interacting out loud, it provides additional information for coaching. If they choose to do it silently, request a sign to let you know when they're finished.

*Is there anything else you need to say to them? Is there anything you need to hear from them? (Coaching may be necessary here but based only on what has been learned from the client.)*

*Let go of all of that poison...and when you've forgiven them completely, they'll just fade out of that chair. Let me know when they're gone.*

Occasionally a part of the person in that chair will refuse to fade. Be ready to dance! I once had a client, Natalie, whose mother-in-law refused to fade completely. Just the face and head remained. Time was running out for the session and...

I wonder if you can store that head someplace safe until the forgiveness is complete. Some place where she won't bother you at all as you finish the work to let go of the anger. Maybe we'll finish next week, maybe you'll finish the forgiveness before then...as you continue letting go completely.

I was surprised that Natalie chose a Tiffany's box to store her mother-in-law's head! From what I'd learned about the woman through Natalie, I might have stored her in a porta-potty with the head facing down into the bowl. But, the metaphor Natalie chose indicated something important. When I inquired about it, she said,

> *I just saw her in a different light. I respect her even if I'm mad at her for hurting my feelings. I'll put her in a Tiffany's box and tie that white ribbon extra tight. And I'll store her on the back porch until we're through.*

On her next visit, Natalie stated she was no longer angry. She said the day before our session, she realized she had a few more things to say to her mother-in-law, and a few things to thank her for, so she untied the ribbon and opened the box. Natalie said the head was gone. (Realization is simply consciously understanding what the subconscious has already worked out.) Natalie said that was the best gift she'd ever gotten in a Tiffany's box.

It was a pretty darn good gift for me too because I knew Natalie was discovering the power of self-hypnosis and her imagination. The empty chair can be used for things other than forgiveness. You're limited only by the limitations of your own imagination. (Handout available at KarenHand.com/Trance-Dance)

In the demo with Janet, she said she wanted to erase self-doubt. Thus, the metaphor with the large pink eraser. Erasing was her idea! It also seemed prudent to reconnect her to her own unique perfection. So, a quick regression journey to a younger time and her inner child. Since Janet indicated she was externally motivated, it seemed to help to have that little one for whom she could work. And there were some reframing and perceptual changes along the way. The formal hypnosis repeats what was learned and installs or solidifies the action steps to change.

I prefer the least invasive approach first! And this demo indicates how a change might occur even while specifying what one really wants. I start with the Outcome Specification "Intervention" and wide-awake hypnosis. Once I have a specific desire for the session, we wrap up by strengthening the epiphanies and self-acceptance in "formal trance" and emerge with the belief of easily reaching that goal. Additional sessions are scheduled if necessary.

Six months after that demonstration in a conference workshop, Janet texted me about her progress:

*"I am way more confident and this year has opened up for me to do more presentations (was on my bucket list but thought no one would care about what I had to share). I was keeping a wins journal too for a while but quit. So, for effectiveness, 5 stars out of 5!"*

There doesn't seem to be much lingering self-doubt! This is "proof" that something this simple can have profound results. Janet is speaking at several hypnosis conferences in person and online this year. So, the feedback indicates, at least in this example, that simply using the "Outcome Specification Intervention" with free-style wide-awake hypnosis followed by some direct suggestion accomplished the desired result.

When the outcome is clearly specified, positive in nature, accomplishable, and believable, a change can be chunked down enough to realize the difference. And then, if more work is necessary to expand the results, you'll have a good indication of what needs to be done on subsequent visits.

See your client in the best possible light. Believe they can achieve their goal. Use curiosity to discover how they are running a behavior app (that they downloaded for a positive reason at some point), and then apply your best techniques to affect the change they desire. The dance can be a beautiful thing to experience. And remember, you are not changing them into a dancer. You are finding the steps that brings out the best in your partner. If they become a dancer along the way, their life will be enriched even more.

Now, just like in Dancing with the Stars, the show and the partnership eventually come to an end. In the change or persuasive communication business, you'll know the dance is successful when your partner is empowered to manage their own dance even when they're dancing with new issues in their future.

CHAPTER 13:

# THE FINAL BOW

Looking back over the changes I've made over the years in how I run a session (and my business), there's one thing that's very clear. The longer I do this, the less I do.

I remember the days when I spent an immense amount of time before ever meeting a client:

- Looking for the script with the right "magic" words
- Scouring google for as much information as I could gather on their issue
- Asking colleagues how they would handle a particular problem
- Reading books on metaphor to find the right analogy
- Taking class after class trying to convince myself I knew enough to solve the problems of any client who walked in the door

- Driving myself to stress and distraction trying to be perfect in all things!

Finally, after seeing hundreds of clients, using a wide variety of scripts and "foolproof" techniques, and reviewing both successes and failures, I had the epiphany. When I'm really present with my client, and when I listen and watch carefully what the client is saying (and not saying) and when I'm curious about how they think those thoughts, I'll discover their behavior chain: Trigger—Thought—Action—Consequence. Then I can help them map their strategy for success. Change anything in the chain and there will be a difference.

Abraham Lincoln was right when he said, "You can fool all of the people some of the time; you can fool some of the people all of the time, but you can't fool all of the people all of the time."

It's the same with hypnosis. I don't care how good or how savvy you are as a hypnotist, you won't hypnotize all of the clients all of the time. But you can certainly increase your success quotient when you look and listen carefully to the client who is in front of you (maybe take notes) and then trust that you will offer the best service your training has prepared you to offer.

I learned a long time ago from Jason Linett (one of the best in the hypnosis industry) that one must also be a "business-person" to succeed as an entrepreneur. He taught me to work smarter, not harder. I take a business-like frame when it comes to attracting and accepting new clients.

I model Jason, and I use my 3-point plan for success:

1. **Know Yourself** – It doesn't really matter if you're a buttoned-up, suit-wearing professional or a tie-dyed, fringe-wearing sound healer. Know what you do, own it and present it to the world authentically to the best of your ability. Your tribe (like-minded seekers) will find you.

I happen to like "kitschy" hypnosis things and wear jewelry and have tchotchkes to show it. Anyone who is turned off by that when they see me in person or on my website will not become my client. And that's fine, that's not my business. People who do resonate with the games I play and the smile I flash WILL super-select themselves into a screening. I have qualified clients from all over the world who choose to make that request.

2. **Know Your Outcome** – Every persuasive communicator has an outcome in mind. As a hypnotist, your job is not to push whatever outcome you think the client should have, but to facilitate the outcome the client has in mind. If you can't go along with their outcome, don't take them as a client!

   Be aware, your client may have plenty of people in their life who are "shoulding" all over them. Avoid that choir. Listen to your client to really understand what <u>they</u> want, then facilitate <u>that</u> outcome. As you are successful, they will leave happy and return when they're ready to make another change. They are likely to send you referrals too.

3. **Know Your Audience** – Use the NLP Presuppositions to form the framework around your client and see them as successful. Then tailor your suggestions, scripts, and techniques to each individual client by using their words and their desires and by breaking up their limiting beliefs. If you're talking to a child (even an inner child), use age-appropriate language and stories plus tone, tempo, volume, etc. If you're talking to someone who has a flip-phone and doesn't own a computer, skip the high-tech analogies and use something more relevant instead. You want your client to experience success so you might as well make it as easy as possible to help them accomplish that success.

When it comes to business, once you have a clear profile of your ideal client, current styles and trends will help you know where to go to reach them. Use the Meta Pattern model if you need a template for writing a pitch or an ad. Always be authentic and keep putting yourself out there.

Back when I was a professional in the radio broadcasting field, I advised students to pick five cities in which they'd like to live and send their audition tape to every program director in those markets. When you cover enough ground, you will find people who line up with what you do. It's a strategy that has worked in all of my endeavors. And when your strategy is to build clientele, be authentic, tell as many people as you can reach in your area of interest, and be responsive. You too will find the people who resonate with your style.

I stopped doing free in-person consultations and started doing free 30-minute phone or Zoom screenings. Changing that one word changed the quality of my clients. I no longer "convince" prospects that hypnosis will help them. I SCREEN prospects to discover if they qualify for what I offer. If not, I refer them to a qualified colleague or explain what has to be done to meet the requirements for a session with me. And honestly, because I'm completely transparent in my public presentation, I rarely get an unqualified client requesting an appointment.

Hypnosis happens every day in every way when hypnosis is allowed to happen. Be the best you that you can be and realize you ARE a hypnotist! If you can imagine it, you can make it happen. You have to go there first and your client will follow. It's the Trance Dance, the hypnotic art of leading and following. Keep those dancing shoes on and enjoy!

Thank you for doing this dance with me.

For a copy of techniques, handouts and videos mentioned in this book, go to KarenHand.com/Trance-Dance.

# CURTAIN CALL

I want to first acknowledge my husband, Mark Harper, who is my rock and continues to offer support as I continue to reinvent myself. Appreciation goes to my daughter, Jessica Graham, who is my cheerleader. I have deep gratitude for my Hypno teachers, colleagues and friends: Dr. Patrick Porter, Michael Watson, Jason Linett, Shawn and Sarah Carson, Jess Marion, Larry Garrett, Carm Blacconiere, Robert and Linda Otto, Linda Williamson, Shelley Stockwell-Nicholas, Laney Coulter, Melissa Roth, Catherine Johns, and Sandra Madison. Plus, a special shoutout to Suzy Day and Wendie Webber for title assist and Judy Waddick for the cover art. I am most grateful to my amazing editor Kelly Joy Simmons who is my very own Michelangelo.

And I hold in very high esteem the International Association of Counselors and Therapists for being a leader in the evolution of Hypnosis. Plus, I'm professionally indebted to the "non-denominational" conventions, the Mid-America Hypnosis Conference and HypnoThoughts Live, for welcoming and respecting all of the various styles of hypnosis and opening the minds of many to the reality that hypnosis happens, ready or not!

## ABOUT THE AUTHOR

Karen Hand is a Board-Certified Hypnotist, Trainer, International Best-Selling author, and World-Class Communicator. Her 30-year career as a Chicago radio personality was the perfect foundation for using language to help others exercise their imagination. Karen's transition to Hypnosis re-purposed that skill set and since 2005 she has helped thousands of people take control of their lives and she's trained countless hypnotists and NLPers to help others change for good. Karen sees clients and conducts trainings in her Chicago office and globally via ZOOM. She has received many awards including: Hypnotist of the Year, Educator of the Year, Leadership Award, and the IMDHA Pen & Quill Award for Literary Excellence.

Karen is the author of the best-selling book *Magic Words and Language Patterns, The Hypnotist's Essential Guide to Crafting Irresistible Suggestions*, and *Hypnotic Workshops Like a Pro!*, co-written with Kelley T. Woods.

Made in the USA
Monee, IL
17 November 2021

82343881R00085